SPECIAL EDUCATION SERIES
Peter Knoblock, *Editor*

Achieving the Complete School:
Strategies for Effective Mainstreaming
Douglas Biklen
with Robert Bogdan, Dianne L. Ferguson,
Stanford J. Searl, Jr., and Steven J. Taylor

Stress in Childhood:
An Intervention Model for Teachers and Other Professionals
Gaston E. Blom, Bruce D. Cheney,
and James E. Snoddy

Curriculum Decision Making for Students with Severe Handicaps:
Policy and Practice
Dianne L. Ferguson

Helping the Visually Impaired Child with Developmental Problems:
Effective Practice in Home, School, and Community
Sally M. Rogow

Progress Without Punishment:
Effective Approaches for Learners with Behavior Problems
Anne M. Donnellan, Gary W. LaVigna,
Nanette Negri-Shoultz, and Lynette L. Fassbender

Issues and Research in Special Eduation, Volumes 1 and 2
Robert Gaylord-Ross, Editor

Cultural Diversity, Families, and the Special Education System:
Communication and Empowerment
Beth Harry

Interpreting Disability: A Qualitative Reader
Philip M. Ferguson, Dianne L. Ferguson,
and Steven J. Taylor, Editors

On Being L.D.:
Perspectives and Strategies of Young Adults
Stephen T. Murphy

Toward Effective Public School Programs for Deaf Students:
Context, Process, and Outcomes
Thomas N. Kluwin, Donald F. Moores, and Martha Gonter Gaustad,
Editors

Communication Unbound:
How Facilitated Communication Is Challenging
Traditional Views of Autism and Ability/Disability
Douglas Biklen

Facilitated Communication Training
Rosemary Crossley

Facilitated Communication Training

Rosemary Crossley

Teachers College, Columbia University
New York and London

Photographs by Helen Graham

Published by Teachers College Press, 1234 Amsterdam Avenue, New York, N.Y. 10027

Library of Congress Cataloging-in-Publication Data

Crossley, Rosemary, 1945–
  Facilitated communication training / Rosemary Crossley.
    p.   cm. — (Special education series; 14)
  Includes bibliographical references and index.
  ISBN 0-8077-3327-X (paper)
    1. Communicative disorders—Patients—Rehabilitation.
  2. Communication devices for the disabled. 3. Handicapped—Means of communication. I. Title. II. Series: Special education series
  (New York, N.Y.); 14.
  RC429.C76   1994
  616.89'8206516—dc20   93-44306

ISBN 0-8077-3327-X

Printed on acid-free paper
Manufactured in the United States of America
01 00 99 98 97 96 95 94 93   8 7 6 5 4 3 2 1

Dedication

To Chris Borthwick, who, as ever, did all the cooking, and to Anne McDonald, who lived through it.

Contents

Acknowledgments

The development of a systematic program of facilitated communication training from my original use of facilitation with children with cerebral palsy owes a great deal to the staff who have worked at the DEAL Communication Center since 1986, and whose names are listed in alphabetical order below. Those staff whose names are asterisked also made significant contributions to some of the working papers on which this book is based. Any errors in the text are, of course, my own.

DEAL STAFF 1986–1992

*Jim Allen
*Margaret Batt
*Anne Burke
Jenny Denning
Anne Doherty
Helen Graham
Jane Jones
Jenny Lambier
Lindsay Low
Jean Melzer
Alan Moore
Sean O'Connor
Alice Owens
Elizabeth Pearson
*Jane Remington-Gurney
*Sue Rushfirth
Rosemary Ryall
Sue Vincent

Special thanks go to Nancy O'Donnell A.M., Jane Remington-Gurney (now Advisor, Facilitated Communication, Queensland Department of Family Services), Doug Biklen and all at the Facilitated Communication Training Institute of Syracuse University, Graeme Clunies-Ross, Joan Dwyer, Carl Parsons, Michael Regos, and John Warburton.

The DEAL Committee of Management, and private and public benefactors, all gave essential support and encouragement despite the controversies that facilitated communication produced. And a facilitated communication program could not exist without facilitators—those parents, caregivers, integration support teams, and training center staff who, despite all difficulties, gave their help ungrudgingly to people with severe communication impairments.

Lastly, but never least, are the DEAL clients, each one of whom taught us something. These are the people we hoped to help, either through traditional nonspeech communication or through facilitated communication training. Sadly not all have been helped, either because our skills were not equal to the task, or because of unwillingness on the part of others to recognize their abilities and their right to a means of communication.

Some of the material in this book is based on articles originally published in *American Journal of Speech Pathology* and *Topics in Language Disorders* and I thank the editors of these journals for their assistance.

Introduction

＊——＝◆＝——＊

COMMUNICATING WITHOUT SPEECH

In *The Count of Monte Cristo* Dumas (1845) described a man who had lost speech and writing skills following what would now be diagnosed as a brain stem stroke but who was still able to communicate by using eye movements to accept or reject letters and words spoken by his daughter. This may be the first recorded use of a communication system by a person with severe communication impairment unrelated to hearing loss. Prior to the 1970s such communication strategies were rare, and those that were used were generally, as in Dumas, devised by families and caregivers to suit one individual. Only recently have there been attempts to develop widely applicable communication techniques for people with severely impaired speech and hand function. When McNaughton began teaching children with severe physical impairments, in 1968, little provision was made for those who could not speak: "the odd lucky child received a wheelchair tray, with magazine pictures related to basic needs" (McNaughton, 1990).

Seminal work in nonspeech communication was carried out in the early 1970s when protocols for the use and design of communication boards were devised (McDonald & Schultz, 1973; Vicker, 1974), and Blissymbols were used successfully by children with cerebral palsy in Canada from 1971 (McNaughton & Kates, 1980). The new field acquired a title, augmentative and alternative communication, and its own terminology (Appendix A). Augmentative communication is used to augment speech that is limited in vocabulary or intelligibility. Alternative communication is used instead of speech, where speech is either absent or totally unintelligible. Both

1

augmentative and alternative communication involve the same equipment and strategies.

Developments in technology, and in the theory of nonspeech communication, were taking place at the same time. The Canon Communicator, a minitypewriter designed in Holland for people with dual sensory impairments, was speedily taken up by people with severe communication impairments, as had been the Possum scanning typewriter, designed in England for people who could not use their hands to type. Augmentative communication, like many other fields of human endeavor, was given a tremendous boost by the sale of the first personal computers, in 1975, and since then the increasing miniaturization of electronic components and developments in voice output technology have led to the production of many new devices, catering to people with a range of academic and physical abilities.

Most work in augmentative communication was initially directed toward assisting people with severe physical impairments such as cerebral palsy, and the aids and strategies developed reflected this. People who were unable to point with their hands directly to communication displays were accommodated by using eye pointing, headpointers, or manual or switch-controlled scanning systems. Large communication displays or eye-pointing charts were mounted on wheelchairs, to be followed in the 1980s by laptop computers and speech synthesizers.

Individuals with severe communication impairments are often falsely labeled as intellectually impaired, not surprising when one considers how the standard categorization of intellectual impairments, the Diagnostic and Statistical Manual of Mental Disorders, bases its categorizations on expressive language skills. In the 1970s relatively little was done to provide the technology or techniques to help this group, most of whom are ambulatory. Even for many professionals the image of the augmentative communication user appeared to be that of a person with an able mind trapped in a disabled body.

While generally augmentative communication catered specifically to the needs of intellectually able, literate individuals with severe physical impairments and severe communication impairments, an exception to this trend occurred in Britain. There, three speech therapists, Cornforth, Johnson, and Walker (1974), developed a communication training program using manual signing for people with hearing impairments who had been assessed as having severe learning difficulties. Sign language programs using their

Makaton vocabulary were widely implemented and have been successful in providing some functional communication for many students with a range of developmental disabilities. Communication through signing requires communication partners who know the signs, and is not functional for students who have severe hand function impairments or who have difficulty replicating the signs.

More recently, communication displays using Blissymbols and other pictorial systems have been used successfully by some people diagnosed as intellectually impaired. This has been followed by the development of smaller, cheaper voice-output aids with utterances coded by pictures or symbols. An intrinsic problem with picture or symbol-based displays is the limited vocabulary available. Aid use has also not been functional for individuals who have had problems accurately selecting items from large displays.

Despite all the developments in nonspeech communication strategies and technology over the last 20 years, there is still a substantial number of individuals who have not yet achieved fluent, functional communication with any of the available systems. Some of these people may be helped by facilitated communication training.

FACILITATED COMMUNICATION TRAINING

Facilitated communication training is a strategy for teaching individuals with severe communication impairments to use communication aids with their hands. In facilitated communication training a partner (facilitator) helps the communication aid user overcome physical problems and develop functional movement patterns. The facilitator uses his or her hand(s) to support or inhibit the aid user. The immediate aim is to allow the aid user to make choices and to communicate in a way that had been previously impossible. Practice, using a communication aid such as a picture board, speech synthesizer, or keyboard in a functional manner, is encouraged to increase the user's physical skills and self-confidence and reduce dependency. As the student's skills and confidence increase the amount of facilitation is reduced. The ultimate goal is for students to be able to use the communication aids of their choice independently.

Facilitated communication training is a teaching strategy of particular relevance to individuals with severe speech impairments who can walk but have had difficulty acquiring handwriting and manual signing skills. Many such people are diagnosed as autistic and/or intellectually impaired. Through facilitated communication training many of these people have achieved functional communication, often revealing unexpected understanding and academic potential.

My initial use of facilitated communication had no theoretical basis: It was a measure forced upon me by circumstances. After teaching children with cerebral palsy for 5 years, in 1977 I started to try and devise a means of communication for a socially responsive 16-year-old with athetoid cerebral palsy and no intelligible speech, who had been labeled profoundly intellectually impaired.

Anne had been living in a state institution since she was 3, and was still the size of a 3-year-old. She had no wheelchair and lay on the floor during the day. Severe extensor spasm had caused her body to arch in a bow shape, with her head pushed backwards toward her heels. When she was seated in a baby buggy (a larger version of a baby's stroller, and the only seating available) her head and shoulders retracted to the extent that she was at risk of suffocation. In order for her to look at anything placed in front of her it was necessary to flex her hips forcibly and bring her head forward. In order for her to point it was necessary to use my hand to internally rotate her arm and raise it from its retracted position behind her. With this support Anne pointed correctly to named objects, pictures, and a few Blissymbols before going on to learn to read and spell.

Anne left the institution at the age of 18, still in the baby buggy, after instructing a lawyer and winning an action for Habeas Corpus in the Supreme Court of Victoria. Now in her senior year at university, Anne still uses facilitated communication. For her it is a matter of choice:

> I communicate by spelling on an alphabet board, on which I can reach a top speed of 400 words an hour. I own a Canon Communicator... which I use with a headpointer...; a speech synthesizer...and a computer which...is the slowest to use of all my high-tech communication equipment.... I can type at 10 words an hour, provided someone else sets up the computer.... The gadgets enable me to do things I can't do without them, but they don't let me do them fast enough to make it worthwhile. If technology made me normal, it would be great;

as it is it makes me slower and less efficient
and reduces the time I would otherwise spend
with non-disabled people. (Harrington, K. A
letter from Annie, *Communicating Together*,
1988)

In Anne's case facilitation produced only minimal physical improvement. For her, independence could only come through alternate means of access, a headpointer or switches, that she found unsatisfactory. There will always be some people who can only communicate with facilitation or who have to choose between restricted or slow independent communication aid use, and dependent, faster, more fluent communication.

While Anne's use of facilitated communication caused considerable local controversy at the time, Anne was certainly not the first individual with such disabilities to have shown academic abilities, and therapists experienced in working with people with cerebral palsy were not surprised that a child with severe cerebral palsy and no speech could have been misassessed and have considerable, untapped potential. However, the use of facilitated communication training with individuals with other diagnoses still arouses controversy. Since the 1960s facilitated communication has been used occasionally with people with autism—Rosalind Oppenheim, in particular, in her book *Effective Teaching Methods for Autistic Children*, which was first published in 1977, articulated a rationale and a program for teaching children with autism to communicate through facilitated handwriting—but until recently it has been applied to only a few individuals.

The development of a training program based on facilitated communication was stimulated by the 1986 opening of DEAL, Australia's first center devoted solely to the needs of individuals with severe communication impairments not caused by deafness. It was expected that the clientele would be largely people with cerebral palsy or acquired brain damage. In fact, from 1986 to 1990, only 213 (32%) of DEAL's 666 clients with developmental disabilities were diagnosed as having a severe physical impairment and 636 (95%) were labeled as either intellectually impaired or autistic or both. Statistics on the incidence of severe communication impairments are limited but it appears that (1) a high proportion of those individuals labeled as severely or profoundly intellectually impaired have severe communication impairments, and (2) the majority of those with severe communication impairments are labeled as intellectually impaired (often in association with other diagnoses such as cerebral palsy or autism). In a statewide survey of all individuals with developmental or acquired severe communication impairments, 71% of all respondents had been labeled as intellectually impaired (Bloomberg & Johnson, 1990).

Of the DEAL clients labeled as intellectually impaired or autistic, two thirds were reported as having some exposure to manual signing programs but only four had acquired more than 100 signs. Of those aged over 10, fewer than 5% could write a simple sentence to dictation, and fewer than 50% could write their names.

During assessment of selection skills, some 90% of the 452 individuals labeled as intellectually impaired who did not have cerebral palsy showed neuromotor problems that adversely affected their ability to make accurate selections from a communication display. The most common were eye/hand coordination impairments, impulsiveness, perseveration, low muscle tone, and inability to isolate an index finger. Facilitation was used when necessary to provide temporary remedies for these problems while academic skills were assessed.

The results of academic assessment were initially surprising—some 70% of the 431 over age 5 showed useful literacy skills, defined as the ability to type a comprehensible sentence without a model, such as "it woz nise." On reflection our surprise diminished. Unlike Anne, most of these people were living in the community and had attended schools; they could all walk and pick up books and magazines, and had considerable exposure to ambient print on television, signs, packaging, and so forth. Their speech and hand function impairments, however, had prevented them from demonstrating any of their acquired literacy skills. Initially all but two of those with previously unused spelling skills required facilitation in order to use keyboards successfully.

The occupational and physical therapists at DEAL suggested strategies that could be used to improve specific hand functions, and the combination of facilitated communication and motor training was called facilitated communication training. Not all users of facilitation have literacy skills; facilitation is also used when necessary to assist individuals accessing symbol and picture boards, or choosing from real objects, such as toys.

Facilitated communication training is far from problem-free. Essentially, it is an ad hoc solution to some of the communication problems of ambulatory school-age children or adults with both severe speech and hand function impairments whose communication cannot be put on hold while they undertake a lengthy occupational therapy program. The most obvious concerns are the dependency that the use of facilitation may produce and the risk of facilitators unduly influencing communication. While some hundreds of individuals have been assisted by facilitated communication training, it is not an ideal strategy—it is the strategy you use when you don't have a better one.

Facilitated communication training has excited attention because the communication produced with facilitation is unexpected in both style and content, and challenges previous assumptions about the language skills of specific groups, especially people with autism. The most important contribution facilitated communication training could make to the field of nonspeech communication would be to bring about the reevaluation of individuals with severe communication impairments who are labeled as intellectually impaired, and a reexamination of the methods used to assess these individuals. Detailed neuromotor assessment of all infants with significant speech delays and early intervention by speech/language pathologists and physical therapists could eradicate the need for facilitated communication training within a generation. In the meantime the findings that led to facilitated communication training should add further impetus to research into the neurological links between speech and hand function.

Meanwhile, the aim of all communication intervention should be free speech. As far as is possible people with severe communication impairments should be enabled to say what they want to say, in the words thay want to use, when and where they want, without restrictions imposed by their communication partners, technology, or the enviroment.

In 1992, Anne McDonald wrote a plea for the right to communicate:

For people without speech, talking is often dependent on the generosity of others, either in providing interpretation or facilitation or in giving up time to listen. While this is inevitable, there needs to be an irreducible right to make your opinions known on issues concerning your future well-being. At the moment social conversation and medical consent are equal in the sight of the law, both depending on the accidental availability of communication partners with the necessary skills and commitment. There is no right to be heard. There is no right to an interpreter. There is no obligation to listen.

While social interactions will always be dependent on the politeness and tolerance of individuals, it should be possible to legislate for a right to communicate in formal situations such as courts, hospitals and schools. Without such legally enforceable rights, people without speech will continue to be at the mercy of decision-makers who can arbitrarily decide to disallow communication.

Communication falls into the same category as food, drink and shelter— it is essential for life. Without communication life becomes worthless.

The aim of this book is to enable more individuals to communicate as freely as possible.

1

Assessment for Facilitated Communication Training

➤ ⊷ ⊷

Facilitated communication training is a strategy for teaching people with severe communication impairments to use communication aids with their hands. It is just one of many strategies for helping people with severe communication impairments, and this chapter aims to place it in the context of the overall field of augmentative and alternative communication and to outline the path that might lead to someone becoming involved in a facilitated communication training program.

SEVERE COMMUNICATION IMPAIRMENT

Individuals are described as having severe communication impairments when their speech and handwriting are insufficient to meet their communication needs. The term is usually used in relation to hearing people with no speech or very little intelligible speech, but it may also be applied appropriately to people whose speech, while clear and fluent, is still not meaningful or representative of their real thoughts.

Many people whose speech is severely impaired also have difficulty with handwriting.

AUGMENTATIVE AND ALTERNATIVE COMMUNICATION

Augmentative and alternative communication is the formal title for the nonspeech communication strategies used by people who are not deaf. Augmentative communication includes any communication strategy needed to make an individual's speech more functional; Jan's family understands her speech but when she's away from home she augments her speech by using a communication book which includes proper names. Alternative communication includes any communication strategy used when a person has no comprehensible speech at all. In fact, the strategies used to augment speech are the same as those used instead of speech. The difference between augmentative and alternative communication is merely the difference between partial and total dependency on nonspeech communication. For simplicity the term augmentative communication is used throughout this book. A list of terms used and their definitions can be found in Appendix A.

Who Needs to Use Augmentative Communication?

Anyone whose speech is not clear enough, fluent enough, or reliable enough to allow them to get across everything they need to say.

What Communication Strategies Can Be Used Instead of Speech?

Speech may be replaced or augmented by:

1. gesture and body language
2. manual sign
3. handwriting
4. communication aids.

Gesture and body language are used to some extent by almost all people. While some formalized gestures, such as nodding the head for "yes" and shaking for "no" are powerful, there are intrinsic limits on the sophistication of communication obtainable by gesture and body language alone. In particular, while a person can respond to questions or circumstances through gesture and body language, initiating and carrying on a conversation is virtually impossible.

Manual sign is as powerful as speech for face-to-face communication, providing all parties to the interaction share extensive sign vocabularies—that is, they can use and understand thousands of signs in the same way as adult speakers use and understand thousands of words. Few people who are not deaf have been exposed to sufficient manual sign to acquire large vocabularies. Consequently manual signing only attains its full power when used in the deaf community.

Handwriting is as powerful as the literacy skills of writer and reader. It loses the inflexion given by speech, sign, and gesture, but it is probably the most common way of compensating for the kinds of speech incapacity caused by acute illness in older children or adults.

Communication aids are devices developed or adapted for use by people with severe communication impairments. Because they have very varied skills, needs, and problems there is a large range of communication aids. Some people with severe communication impairments can use their hands while others cannot, and have to use alternatives such as mouth sticks, headsticks, switches, or eye-pointing. Some can read and spell and others cannot: They need communication aids on which language elements are represented by pictures or symbols. Some individuals use wheelchairs that can accommodate large communication devices; others walk and need small, light aids. Some have the funds to purchase high tech equipment; others do not. A communication aid may be as simple as a piece of cardboard with NO and YES written on it or as complex as a laptop computer controlled with one switch that allows the user to speak on the phone or type an essay.

What Is the Best Nonspeech Communication Strategy?

The best nonspeech communication strategy (or combination of strategies) is the one that allows the person with severe communication impairments to communicate as freely as possible in as many situations as possible to the maximum number of people.

How Is the Best Nonspeech Communication Strategy Selected?

In deciding what strategies are feasible the first thing to consider is what physical abilities the person has. Hand skills are the obvious place to start.

Body language, gesture, and sign language have the advantage that no equipment is needed—they are called unaided strategies. Handwriting needs minimal equipment. However, if communication is to be fluent and comprehensible, these strategies do need good hand skills. Manual sign and handwriting place considerable demands on motor planning and memory as well as on fine finger and hand movements. Unfortunately, many individuals with severe communication impairments have problems in using their hands effectively, and for these people manual signing and handwriting are not realistic options.

A range of communication aid options is available for people with severe communication impairments who do not use their hands at all. Ironically, those with severe communication impairments who use wheelchairs have more communication aid access options than those who walk. Large communication aids and displays that can be mounted on wheelchair trays, access strategies using headpointers, eye-pointing boards, or switch-controlled scanners—all these are feasible for wheelchair users, but impractical for walkers.

People with severe communication impairments who can walk, but cannot sign or write, need small, easily portable communication aids that they are able to use with their hands. The aid displays a set of choices, and the user makes selections from these choices, reducing the demands on fine motor skills, motor planning, and memory.

Academic assessment will determine the items on the display which may include pictures, special symbols such as Blissymbols, written words or phrases, or the letters of the alphabet. The communication aid itself may be an electronic device, with spoken or written output, or it may be a board or a folder that the partner reads the message from as the user constructs it. Whatever the nature of the communication aid or the display used, people who are walking have to use their hands to select the items they want.

At initial assessment many of these people do not have the pointing and selection skills necessary to use communication aids effectively. As they have no other practical communication options—they cannot sign or write, they cannot carry eye-pointing displays, or enlarged keyboards or scanning setups, and they cannot wear headpointers—the only remaining option is to try and teach them the hand skills necessary to use portable communication aids. One teaching strategy that may be used with these individuals is facilitated communication training.

WHAT IS FACILITATED COMMUNICATION TRAINING?

Facilitated communication training is a teaching strategy in which a communication partner (facilitator) helps a communication aid user overcome neuromotor problems and develop functional movement patterns. The immediate aim is to allow the aid user to make choices and to communicate in a way that has been impossible previously. When the student's skills and confidence increase, the amount of facilitation is reduced. The ultimate goal is for students to be able to use the communication aids of their choice independently.

COMMUNICATION AID USE INVOLVING FACILITATION

For facilitated communication training to be considered an option for an individual, he or she will

- have severe communication impairments
- not currently have a fluent alternative communication strategy
- not show the potential to acquire manual signing or hand-writing skills easily[1]
  or
- live in an environment where manual sign or writing are not going to be viable communication options
- have difficulty with the clear, unambiguous selection of nominated items from functional communication displays
- not be able to use other direct or indirect access options (usually for practical reasons, such as the unsuitability of these options for individuals who walk and have to carry their communication systems with them).

Once it has been decided that an individual is a candidate for facilitated communication training it is then necessary to

- ascertain the nature of the problem(s) that currently preclude successful communication aid access
- select appropriate remedial strategies, including facilitation strategies if needed
- ascertain what representational systems (concrete objects, pictures, pictographs, written words, letters) are currently meaningful to the potential user
- enable the individual with severe communication impairments to use the most empowering of the representational systems and selection strategies currently available to him/her by obtaining or making appropriate communication aids and teaching those in the individual's environment how the aids are used.

The individual with severe communication impairments can then practice using a communication aid with facilitation. This is just the start of the training program. Further teaching and assessment in areas such as literacy, hand function, and pragmatic interactive skills, will be required.

If the person with severe communication impairments shows the ability to spell at the initial assessment, further assessment and refinement of literacy skills is desirable. If no usable spelling skills are shown, then the person's involvement in a literacy program is desirable. Spelling is the most empowering communication strategy for people with severe communication impairments who cannot sign fluently, and every effort should be made to develop literacy skills regardless of the presenting diagnosis of the individual with severe communication impairments. Infants and individuals for whom literacy acquisition is problematic will need to be taught to use as large a vocabulary of pictures and symbols as possible.

Given that the individual is using facilitation because of problems with hand use, regular hand function assessments, which may result in the prescription of exercise routines or splints, are important.

Whatever the representational strategy, all aid users will need to be taught acceptable attention-getting strategies and other pragmatic skills, such as how to position themselves so that people they are talking to can best receive their message.

Multiple facilitators will have to be trained: It is important that the user is able to communicate with as many people as possible to avoid dependency on any one. The amount of facilitation provided requires regular review with the aim of reducing it as quickly as possible.

Up to this point I have made no mention of specific labels or of psychological or intellectual assessment. This is because the capacities of people with severe communication impairments cannot be judged until their communication impairments have been addressed. No one should be excluded from communication training because previous intellectual assessments were negative, and no ceiling should be placed on the options offered to individuals because of the labels they wear. Intellectual assessment of people with severe expressive problems is difficult and unreliable. Communication training is a prerequisite for accurate assessment.

ENDNOTE

[1] They may already have tried to sign and write and failed, or the initial assessment may reveal hand function problems that make it unlikely they will acquire fluent signing or writing skills.

2

Facilitated Communication:
How and When

Students whose speech is not adequate for communication have to use other means. Also, students whose fine motor skills are not adequate for acquisition of normal pen and pencil skills need a substitute, usually a keyboard or computer interface. Speech or fine motor skill impairments rapidly become severe educational handicaps if energetic measures are not taken to remedy them. Apart from their day to day effect on the student's classroom performance, these impairments make it extremely difficult to reliably assess a student's actual abilities.

Many students find themselves caught in a downward spiral: Assessed as significantly intellectually impaired as a result of their speech and motor impairments, they are placed in a school where their speech and motor impairments are seen as being the unavoidable corollary of their intellectual impairments. They are unlikely to receive an occupational therapy assessment, and speech therapy is likely to be at a premium. The combined effect of continued failure (after all, the student does not have the basic output skills necessary for success), low expectations, and lack of therapy is likely to be deterioration or stagnation rather than the improvement in skills that is every teacher's aim. The student's behavior is often as poor as their academic performance.

Since the opening of the DEAL Communication Centre in 1986 we have seen many students in this situation. Lyn is one of them. When she first attended DEAL she was 14, diagnosed as autistic, and assessed as having an IQ of 50. Lyn's handwriting was at a first grade level, her muscle tone was low, and she was very impulsive. She had been given training in manual signing and had acquired approximately 100 signs (more than many students, but still much less than the expressive vocabulary of a 2-year-old signer). She used a typewriter with difficulty for simple copying tasks. She was thought to be reading at roughly a 6-year-old level. When facilitated access to a minikeyboard was provided to compensate for Lyn's fine motor problems it quickly became clear that her literacy skills had been significantly under-assessed. Lyn transferred from her special school to a high school and handled the regular syllabus successfully. She is able to type and use her communication aid independently, but had difficulty sustaining the speed and endurance necessary for her heavy academic load without facilitation. Without the initial facilitation Lyn would probably not ever have had access to a regular education.

Because of Lyn's fine motor problems neither signing nor handwriting provided her with an effective alternative to speech. Children who are not succeeding with signing or handwriting, both of which place high demands on fine motor skills, should be reassessed with a view to finding another communication strategy with which they can be more successful. The obvious alternatives all involve making a choice by pointing, either to real objects or to pictures, symbols, words, or letters. These may be used on communication displays, electronic communication aids, or typewriters. The clearest, most effective, pointing is done using the index finger of the preferred hand.

Even though pointing is far less demanding motorically than signing or writing, many students still present problems requiring remediation before accurate pointing is possible. A student's failure to point accurately is all too often seen as a reflection of intellectual impairment or ignorance, and because of this the student's perceptual-motor status is not assessed in detail. After seeing many students similar to Lyn—students who required further communication augmentation, who required intensive manual training to acquire the necessary physical skills, but who were of an age that meant that their educational program had to continue while they had this training—we devised a communication aid access and training program called facilitated communication training.

To facilitate is to make easier. In facilitated communication training the task of using a communication aid is made easier for a student with a severe communication impairment. The degree of facilitation needed varies from person to person, ranging from an encouraging hand on the shoulder to boost confidence, to full sup-

port and shaping of a student's hand to enable isolation and extension of an index finger for pointing.

Facilitation differs from other hands-on training methods such
as coactive movement and graduated guidance. In coactive movements, teachers put their hands over the students' hands and lead
them through a movement pattern. You might, for example, put
your hands over the student's hands and help pull trousers up, or
scoop with a spoon. Coactive movements are performed by both
students and teachers together and it does not matter if the teachers' movements are stronger than that of the students (at least not
at the start of training). In coactive movement you lead the student
through the movement; in facilitated communication you are setting up a situation that will allow the student's own movement to
be functional. It is vital that the choices made be those of the aid
user. The direction of the movement is controlled by the person
being facilitated, not by the facilitator. The aid user's movements
should be stronger than that of the facilitator, who gives the minimum assistance necessary.

Any student whose speech requires augmentation and whose
hand skills are not adequate to achieve a level of expression matching his or her receptive language is a candidate for facilitated communication. Beware of putting the cart before the horse here—as
assessment of students with severe expressive problems is so difficult, no student should be excluded from the training program on
the basis of previous negative assessments. Often the training is a
prerequisite for accurate assessment. Always give the student the
benefit of the doubt. In addition to school students, many adults
with developmental disabilities who can walk have very limited
communication. Their hand function should be carefully assessed.
Faciitation may help those whose hand use is impaired to access
communication aids more successfully.

As facilitated communication requires both hand skills and the
potential to improve those skills, it is not usually the method of
choice for people with severe physical impairments. These people are
offered scanning or coded systems instead. Facilitated communication offers most to students who are ambulatory and who need an
easily portable communication system that can be accessed manually.
To date, successful users of facilitated communication include children diagnosed as intellectually impaired (including children with
Down syndrome), children diagnosed as autistic, and children with
mild cerebral palsy. Regardless of diagnosis, all potential users present
with impairments of motor skills that preclude use of handwriting or

signing for more than the most basic communication, and that significantly impede their independent use of communication aids.

COMMON PROBLEMS HELPED BY FACILITATION

Poor Eye-Hand Coordination

The student makes selections without looking, or without allowing enough time between movements to scan the display and locate the target.

It is vital to ensure that the student makes eye contact with the target before making a selection. The student who points without looking is unlikely to hit the target, and someone who does not scan the available choices cannot make a meaningful selection. At first the facilitator may have to restrain the student from moving until he or she is looking at the target area. Where the student's head is actually turning away from the target the facilitator may need to physically assist in the maintenance of a midline, eyes down, position. If these restrictions are enforced consistently eye/hand coordination usually improves quite rapidly.

Low Muscle Tone

The student's arm and hand are "floppy" or "heavy." There is difficulty raising the arm against gravity and muscles fatigue quickly.

The immediate remedy is to provide some kind of support, adjusted to the aid user. Supports used include the following:

1. The facilitator places hand under aid user's forearm.
2. The facilitator holds the user's sleeve or a wrist band.
3. The user grasps one end of a rod and the facilitator holds the other end.
4 The communication display is positioned so that the user can rest his or her forearm on the table or a typist's support—this is the optimum solution, but only suits users with no other accessing problems and only works while the user is sitting at an appropriate table.

If muscle tone is very poor the student will do best when the aid is positioned as low as possible, minimizing the arm lifting required.

Such students are often more independent in aid use when they are standing up.

Low muscle tone cannot be cured, although it can be increased for short periods. However, it does often go with reduced muscle strength—people with low muscle tone may not be asked to do much, and may not participate in sport—and something can be done about that. The long term strategy that assists people with low muscle tone increase independence combines practice in aid use with an exercise program for arms and shoulders.

High Muscle Tone

The student's arm feels tense, and movements are often too forceful, either over-reaching the target or pushing the aid away.

Usually the harder the student tries to perform the more muscle tone increases. The arm may begin loose and gradually become rigid. This problem is often associated with impulsivity (see "Impulsivity" below).

High muscle tone cannot be cured, but its effects can be alleviated. Remedies include

1. shaking the student's arm until it feels floppy
2. pointing to a target close to the body between selections, so that the student's elbow is flexed between selections
3. regular pauses to give the muscles a chance to relax.

Index Finger Isolation and Extension Problems

The student has difficulty in extending the first finger while holding back the other fingers. Users with this problem either point with all fingers extended or use the middle finger (which is the longest). Either method makes accurate selection difficult.

This is a very common problem. If you can't isolate a finger you cannot point accurately to a small target, and this makes it difficult to use a keyboard or even to have many choices on your picture-board. Remedies vary with the severity, and include the following:

1. An occasional reminder to keep the other fingers back.
2. Asking the aid user to hold a rod in the palm while pointing to encourage flexion of the unwanted fingers (sometimes

this prompts a reflex grasp in which case the index finger will also flex and the aim will be defeated).

3. Physical molding of the student's hand by the facilitator (usually only done for a short period at the start of a training program). When holding the user's hand the facilitator must take care to avoid all contact with the user's index finger (see Figure 2.1 top). Attempts to support the index finger with the facilitator's hand are counterproductive and should be avoided (see Figure 2.1 bottom).

4. Physically restraining the unneeded fingers—a simple method is to use a snug fitting sock. Make a small hole in its toe for the index finger, pull the sock down firmly over the student's hand so that the other fingers are bent and hold it in place by a piece of ribbon or velcro fixed around the wrist. This is a short-term solution—if pointing does not improve within a month further therapy advice should be sought.

A curved or limp index finger may be too weak to push down a key, and may have to be splinted for a short time or a pointer may have to be substituted in the early stages of training. Meanwhile exercises, such as pushing into a ball of clay, can be used to extend and strengthen the finger. It is generally quite easy to achieve independent finger extension; the use of splints slows this down, and they are very much a last resort. Hand molding, too, should be used for only a short period after the initial assessment. If index finger isolation has not improved in a month, further therapy advice should be sought.

Perseveration

The student makes a selection and continues hitting either that selection or adjacent selections inappropriately.

This is a very common problem, though in people with communication impairments it has often gone undiagnosed. The immediate remedy is to break the pattern and pull the student's hand back to the edge of the table after each selection. Gradually, this movement pattern becomes automatic and students withdraw their own hands after each selection. Sometimes providing an alternate target between the student and the aid can assist in the development of the desired movement pattern (e.g., student makes selection 1, hits red dot on table, makes selection 2, hits red dot, makes selection 3, and so forth).

Figure 2.1. Top: Hand molding—the right way. The facilitator does not touch the user's index finger. *Bottom:* Hand molding—the wrong way. The user's index finger curves around the facilitator's fingers.

Perseveration affects the use of communication aids and creates difficulties with assessment. People who have no speech are often given tests involving pointing, and for a person who has perseveration, these will not provide a fair assessment.

Using Both Hands for a Task Only Requiring One

The student points to two items simultaneously and it is hard to be sure which item (if either) was actually desired.

Every effort should be made to discover which is the student's preferred hand and all one-handed tasks should be performed with this hand. It may be necessary to restrain the other hand for some time or to devise other strategies to keep it out of the way, for example a student may put it in his or her pocket, use it to hold a clutch purse, or even sit on it.

Tremor

Tremor can either be a continuous tremor or an intention tremor, where the hand is stable while at rest but trembles when the person tries to do something (such as point).

Tremor is very difficult to remedy. In the short term, stabilizing the limb (either by the facilitator holding the student's wrist, or by the student holding one end of a rod held by the facilitator) will assist. A long term program may involve the wearing of wrist weights while using the hands or the performance of exercises as suggested by an occupational therapist or physiotherapist. However, this does not work for everybody. Tremor is reduced by pointing against resistance, and is helped by firm backwards pressure on the wrist.

Radial/Ulnar Muscle Instability

The muscles of forearm, wrist, and hand exert unequal pull on the hand or fingers. Sometimes the index finger swerves to one side as the student goes to point, leading to unwanted selections. The most common problem is for the aid user's index finger to swing across in front of the other fingers. Often the hand also drops down from the wrist thus making the tip of the index finger invisible to its owner, who is then pointing blind.

Any remedy that restores the finger to view will help in the short term:

1. The user points as though pretending to shoot with the index finger.
2. The user holds one end of a rod while the facilitator holds the other in such a way as to ensure that the user's hand does not drop or swing away from the target.

3. The facilitator's hand is used to correct the user's wrist and hand position.

An exercise program to strengthen the student's arm and hand muscles is usually necessary to achieve long-term improvement.

Initiation Problems

The student does not spontaneously reach out to the communication display.

Some people find it very difficult to initiate a movement. A tap on the shoulder may be necessary before they can get up from a chair. As one person spelled out, "I know what you want me to do, but I just can't get it to happen."

A verbal prompt such as "Do you have something to say?" may be all that is required to start communication, though in the earlier stages a physical prompt such as a touch on the elbow is often necessary. It is important that the communication display is always readily accessible, and that any spontaneous movement toward it is reinforced with a positive response.

Impulsivity

The student moves too fast to produce considered responses—starts pointing at the answer before you've finished the question, or points quickly all over the board so that you don't know which item was meant.

This is frequently, but not necessarily, associated with poor eye/hand coordination and the remedy is similar. Slow the student down and refuse to allow any selections made without looking. Maintain a slight backwards pressure, so that the student is always having to push against your resistance to reach the communication display. (This is good practice with all facilitated students other than those with significantly lowered muscle tone, as the resistance has a stabilizing effect and reduces the chance of the communication partner unintentionally directing the user to a selection.) Pull the hand back after each selection.

Proximal Instability

The student's shoulder and trunk position is unstable. Often an overarm pointing action, rather than the more controlled underarm action, is used.

If you want accurate finger pointing you must have the shoulder, which is the origin of the arm movement, properly stabilized. People with muscle weakness often don't have sufficient stability at the shoulder to allow accurate hand movements. A number of exercises can strengthen shoulder muscles. In the short term firm pressure on the shoulder or on the outside of the upper arm may assist. Seating that encourages a stable, upright posture is also important.

Reduced Proprioception

The student moves awkwardly, sometimes undershooting and sometimes overshooting the target.

Proprioception is the sense that lets us know where the parts of our bodies are in space. To make an accurate movement it is necessary to know where you are starting from and to get feedback from your body as the movement proceeds. Reduced proprioceptive feedback is hard to diagnose with certainty, especially in a person with severe communication impairments. Apparently purposeless movements, such as rocking, that increase proprioceptive feedback *may* indicate that an individual has reduced proprioception. Often diagnosis follows treatment—a girl without any other obvious problems improved her pointing significantly when she wore wrist weights. In lieu of any other obvious explanation, it is presumed that the weights gave her more feedback on the position of her hand and arm. Anything that highlights arm and shoulder position will help—weights, pressure, massage.

Lack of Confidence

While not itself a physical problem nervousness certainly affects physical performance. The most common symptom is reluctance to respond, often combined with lowered muscle tone and reduced eye contact. Encouragement and success are the most effective remedies.

For ease of reference a shorter list of hand function impairments is included in Appendix B.

N.B. For most people with hand function impairments, using a communication aid will be easier if the aid is tilted rather than lying flat on a table.

MOVING TOWARD INDEPENDENCE

The time needed to achieve independent use of a communication aid is influenced by the severity of the problems with which the student started, the motivation of the student, and the availability of skilled, sympathetic, communication partners. As in learning any physical skill, regular practice is vital. (It is probably not coincidental that the students who have moved most rapidly toward independence are those who have transferred into mainstream schools where they have had integration aides available to act as facilitators and pressure to match the quantity of work produced by the other students.)

As soon as a student starts to overcome a problem the assistance given to correct that problem is reduced; for example, a child with very low muscle tone may start communicating with a facilitator giving support under the wrist. With practice, the child's muscles strengthen and the facilitator withdraws support to the forearm. The next step may be to hold the child's elbow, or to lightly hold the sleeve. Whatever the individual variation, the aim is always to withdraw support gradually so that the student continues communicating successfully without loss of confidence.

Students often feel the need for physical contact beyond the time when this is strictly necessary to remedy physical problems. It is important that this need for emotional support is accepted. If it is not, the student may withdraw and stop communicating and the gains made will be lost. A hand on the shoulder usually suffices till this too is gradually faded and the student makes selections without any physical contact from a facilitator. Of course, verbal encouragement is important throughout the whole training procedure and may be necessary even when physical contact is no longer required.

It is important to understand that an aid user's need for facilitation will vary. When tired or unwell many aid users have reduced physical control and may need more support than usual. Also, an aid user's skills will be affected by nervousness, so a student who does not require any physical contact when communicating in a small group, may need a hand on the shoulder when communicating in public. Often aid users who are starting to communicate with new partners initially appear to regress, seeking a degree of support that may have been discontinued months ago with other partners. This must be accepted if the interaction is to progress. Support can be rapidly faded once confidence is established. Some aid users who can type independently, but slowly, find that they can type much more quickly with physical contact. This is a problem in the secondary classroom where both speed and independence are highly desirable and each situation needs to be resolved individually. In the long term speed will improve with practice. Reducing support is discussed in detail in chapter 7.

LITERACY

Facilitation in itself is not directly connected with typing or literacy. It is a means of training manual selection skills that can be used in any situation in which making choices is necessary—selecting a chocolate from a box, choosing an item from a menu, shopping in a supermarket, pointing to body parts on a doll, matching pictures, and so forth. All of these activities require similar eye/hand skills. Nonetheless, many of the users of facilitated communication are using keyboards and this has been an exciting and unexpected outcome of this program.

Most students who have attended DEAL have had considerable exposure to written language, if not to formal literacy training. However, like Lyn, expressive impairments have prevented any literacy skills they have acquired from being recognized. A 16-year-old named Joe used a typewriter with facilitation to show that he could read and spell. His mother said "Now I know why he takes his father's paper every night!" Many teachers and parents report that students were showing an interest in written material—notices, books, papers, magazines, TV commercials—that they found inexplicable until the students found a means of expression, via facilitated communication training, that enabled them to reveal that they had acquired reading skills. For this reason it is important that students be given open-ended assessments when they enter a communication program and not be prejudged on the basis of previous performance or labels. Literacy is discussed in more detail in chapter 4.

3

Structuring Success

⊷ ⊱⊰ ⊶

DEVELOPING SKILLS IN COMMUNICATION BY SPELLING

Successful communication, in whatever mode, has three basic requirements.

First, the sender of the message must have the necessary skills. If the communication is via speech, for instance, the speaker must be able to attract the listener's attention, speak clearly and loudly enough to be heard, and have a vocabulary adequate for the message they want to transmit.

Second, the receiver of the message must have a matching set of skills. If the communication is spoken the listener must pay attention, be able to hear (or lipread), and be able to understand the speaker's language.

Third, the total interaction must facilitate the passage of information. In spoken communication, adaptation to the environment may be necessary—you stand closer to your partner and speak more loudly if there is a lot of background noise. The tone of voice and vocabulary have to match the situation as well as the message content. "Quick march!" on the parade ground will generally have a different intonation from "hurry up" addressed to a child, though the two messages have a similar intention.

These three requirements apply to nonspeech communication as much as to spoken communication; however, fulfillment in nonspeech communication has special problems. We learned our sending, receiving, and interactive skills for social communication when we were very young, and because of this we had two advantages—we were unpressured (nobody worried if we made "mistakes") and we were immersed in a learning environment: Everyone we came into contact with, apart from other infants, had all these skills, and they automatically provided us with appropriate models and reinforcements.

A person starting to use nonspeech communication as an older child or adult is in a very different situation. We tend to be more judgmental of people as they (and we) get older, and the learner is likely to be aware of this and have a well-developed fear of failure. In addition, the learner is not immersed in a learning environment—almost the reverse. The people whom the learner comes in contact with may be unfamiliar with the whole notion of nonspeech communication and are likely to be learning to use the learner's new communication aid or system at the same time he/she is. Correspondingly, the receivers require as much training as the learner does. We are frequently asked why "Joe" doesn't communicate as well outside the therapy setting as he does at DEAL. Generally the answer relates to requirements two and three—the receiver's skills and the interactive strategies used—as much as it does to Joe's lack of confidence in using his new skills and equipment outside the "protected" therapy situation.

The only way communication aid users can communicate exactly what they want to say, in the words they want to use, is by spelling. Consequently every effort is made to develop aid users' spelling skills. Often spelling will be used in conjunction with another communication mode, such as symbols or signing, to increase speed, but the spelling is vital for true freedom of expression.

If Joe is just starting to use spelling for communication there is a hierarchy of activities that can be used to develop the access and spelling skills (and confidence) Joe needs for free communication, while at the same time Joe's communication partners develop their receiving and interactive skills in what is a new situation for everyone (see Figure 3.1).

This ladder is read and "climbed" from the bottom to the top, with the most predictable, most structured activities at the bottom. We have found that both people starting to use keyboards or letterboards and new facilitators more easily achieve successful interactions when the situation is highly structured and only a small number of responses is possible. This generally applies regardless of the academic skills or age of the individuals involved.

It should be emphasized that this is not a rigid structure to be proceeded through step by step. People may do a range of activities in the same session, they may never do some of the activities, and

Figure 3.1. Climbing the ladder: Activities leading to free communication by spelling.

↑	*Self-initiated conversation*—where the users get their aid or ask for it without any prompt.
↑	*Spontaneous conversation*—where the topic is chosen by the user.
↑	*Wide-ranging conversation*—encouragement to use a range of sentence structures may still be necessary (e.g., "Now you ask me a question.").
↑	*Answering questions*—"What did you do at the weekend?" or "How did you like the movie?"
↑	*Typing sentences in a set context*—picture captions, describing pictures, speech balloons for cartoons.
↑	*Exercises with a limited range of answers*—"Give me a word that rhymes with 'day'," or "Give me the opposite of 'big'," or playing the game "Elephant."
↑	*Completing common sentences or phrases*—"Fish and _____" or "Too many cooks spoil _____."
↑	*Cloze exercises*—"Put the missing word in the sentence, Bob _____ a car."
↑	*Exercises with set answers known to the receiver*—crosswords, general knowledge questions, names of friends or family.
↑	*Typing set words*—"Spell 'horse'"; or labeling household items or pictures.
↑	*Copy typing*—"The quick brown fox jumps over the lazy dog."
↑	*Replacing missing letters in words*—perhaps on the Talking Lesson One or Speak and Spell computer toys.
↑	*Word matching*—Bingo, Lotto, word association games (group activity only)
↑	*Yes/no, true/false, and multiple choice*—simple quizzes, "Do dogs go meow?"; "Type C if you want coffee and T if you want tea."

they may be doing highly structured activities with one partner and communicating relatively freely with another. The only rule is that if an attempt at interaction at one level fails, drop down a level or two.

Once initial success is achieved, individuals should always be encouraged to extend their range of activities, regardless of the amount of physical facilitation (if any) they are receiving. Some aid users are communicating freely and fluently while still receiving wrist support. Others require no physical facilitation but still need to build their skills and confidence by rote spelling tasks. Also it does not matter if the aid used is an alphabet board or a computer, the skills required are similar.

When you start to reduce the level of physical support it is often a good idea to go back to a more structured activity, one in which the person is confident of success. A general rule, in fact, is that if the pressure on the person typing is increased in any way—new staff, spectators, reduced facilitation, ill-health, whatever—reduce the level of task in order to maintain success. As the communication impairments of many people are worsened by their lack of self-confidence the aim is always to set the aid user up for success, and not to expose them to any avoidable failures.

It is important that the content of the activity be varied to suit the age and interests of the person: A child may enjoy a crossword about toys, a young man one about cars, and a young woman one about pop stars. Each person requires the same degree of structure but the content and level of difficulty can still vary.

It should be remembered that the list of activities is concerned solely with the development of spelled communication. It is not a complete list of communication behaviors. It ignores body language and eye contact, for instance, two vital communication skills we need to monitor in ourselves and our students.

4

Literacy—Caught or Taught?

━━ ⊰✦⊱ ━━

Reading is surrounded by a number of myths:

1. *Reading is a skill that can only be acquired through formal teaching.*
2. *It is necessary to be able to talk before you can read.*
3. *Reading requires higher intelligence than does understanding speech.*
4. *Someone who cannot write, cannot read.*

SPEAKING AND READING

No one teaches a baby to speak. The baby learns from exposure. People make sounds around the baby and, amazingly quickly, the baby attaches meaning to those sounds. The baby starts to understand what the people around it are saying at about the same time as it starts to imitate the sounds they make. Eventually, any neurologically intact baby will learn to speak the language in which it has been immersed.

Those of us who learn to speak as babies have no memory of the process. Because learning to speak and understand speech is a baby skill, a skill achievable with a mental age of 1, we overlook how enormously complex it is. Think of it! Think of all the different voices, volumes, intonations, and accents the infant is exposed to, not to mention the range of utterances and vocabularies. You say "puss," I say "cat," Nan says "pussycat," Sis says "kitty," and so on. The baby has to work out that we're all talking about the same animal, otherwise known as "Fluff," and the baby has to work it out quickly. Spoken language doesn't hang around. Once spoken it's gone, and the baby can't say "I beg your pardon."

No hard evidence exists as to how much speech a baby needs to hear in order to start to decode speech, but our language decoders are obviously very efficient instruments. After all, most babies understand quite a lot of spoken words at 1 year, and they've spent a lot of that year sleeping. Even when they were awake they were unlikely to have people talking to them all the time.

The intrinsic differences between spoken and written language are the modes of transmission and reception. Speech is heard and print viewed. Speech is produced with the mouth and written language with the hands. Speech is auditory and print visual. There is no intrinsic neurological reason why visual language should be more difficult to acquire than auditory language.

One hundred and fifty years ago written language was a second language, learned after speech, with deliberate effort. As the teaching of reading followed the acquisition of speech, it was assumed that the one was necessary for the other, that is, that children could not learn to read until (and unless) they could talk. This view was held despite the existence of numerous deaf people who, following on the example of the Abbé de l'Epeé[1], had been taught to read despite their lack of speech. Obviously children who cannot speak cannot read aloud. That does not mean that they cannot decode and understand written material, reading silently (as most of us do most of the time).[2]

Reading aloud is the translation of language from the visual mode to the aural mode—it has nothing to do with comprehension of written language, but depends on a knowledge of the relationships between the written and spoken forms of the language. This has become clearer since the development of the first speech synthesizers, in the 1970s. These translate written text into speech using text to speech algorithms that link specific sounds with specific combinations of letters. Their accuracy, at least in reading written English aloud, depends not only on the algorithms but on the length of the exception tables included with the algorithms. Written English is only partially a phonetic representation of spoken English and for a speech synthesizer to read written English aloud accurately it needs to have access to long lists of words whose pronunciation does not follow a rule such as "trough," "through," "tough," "thought," and "though." It is learning the exceptions that makes reading aloud such a difficult task for children to master, a task that may actually distract them from the more important task of extracting meaning from the written language. As the speech synthesizer demonstrates, accurate reading aloud can be achieved with no knowledge of the meaning of the text being read.

Written language has an advantage over spoken language. It stays still. Even on the television screen, those ubiquitous brand names are there for 10 or 20 seconds. If that seems a short time, compare it with the half second it takes to *say* "Coca-Cola." Off the screen, on paper, on the can, it can be looked at again and again. This gives more time for decoding, an advantage for anyone whose processing speed is slower than average.

Forty years ago, before television, junk mail, and supermarkets became universal, there were some children who learned to read before starting school. They were probably children from households where print was valued, where there were books and papers, and where the adults read to the children. Now that virtually every preschool child has considerable print exposure it is likely that the number of children who can read at least some words before they start school will increase.

LEARNING TO READ

Language is language is language—or so it appears. Whatever the differences between Japanese and English, any human child with intact sensory and neurological mechanisms will learn Japanese and English with ease if brought up in a household in which both Japanese and English are spoken. Until recently the written form of English was seen as harder for an English child to learn than spoken Japanese: While it was known that a preschool English-speaking child would pick up Japanese without formal teaching if the child went to live in a Japanese-speaking household, it was still thought that the same child would need to go to school to be taught to read written English.

What is the difference between written English and spoken English, and does the difference explain the difference in method of acquisition? Written English is a visual language and spoken English is an aural language—you look at one, and you listen to the other. There is some relationship between the two, but that in itself has no influence on acquisition methods. There is a relationship between Spanish and Italian, but it has no effect on the acquisition of either in isolation. We know that aural languages can be picked up from exposure—that is the way virtually all human infants learn their native tongues. The important question is—Can visual languages be picked up from exposure? The answer is unequivocally "yes," and it comes not from research on written language but from research on sign language.

The sign languages used in deaf communities are visual languages and infants brought up in households where all or much of the conversation is conducted in manual sign pick up sign language in the same way that infants in speaking households pick up speech. They understand common signs before they can produce them. They "babble" (or fumble) in sign before producing their first recognizable approximations to adult signs. They simultaneously improve their sign production and increase the number of signs they use in the same way as learning speakers improve their articulation and increase their vocabularies.

The evidence indicates that we are equipped to acquire language, not that we are equipped to acquire a particular language or language in a particular mode. Consider the possibility that decoding print can be learned in the same way as decoding speech—that is, from exposure—and that it requires no more academic ability than decoding speech—that is, the ability of a baby. If so, there is no reason to assume that anyone who has the basic prerequisites of adequate eyesight, exposure to meaningful print, and motivation, will not be able to acquire some literacy skills.[3]

The significant difference between written and spoken English that has necessitated different acquisition strategies in the past is not the mode, but the amount of exposure to each mode available in everyday life. Above I said that the relationship between the two was no more significant than the relationship between Italian and Spanish—if you know one language it may make it easier to learn the other, but knowledge of one is not a prerequisite for knowledge of the other. A more illuminating relationship is the relationship between spoken Italian and spoken Latin—both are aural languages; they share many features, but one is usually acquired through exposure and one is only acquired through formal teaching. The difference of course, is the amount of exposure available and its source. In Italy, Italian is spoken wherever you go. While many people know Latin, it is only spoken in special settings, and cannot be learned unless you attend those settings. Italian can be caught, Latin must be taught.[4]

One hundred and fifty years ago, children went to school (if they were lucky) to learn to read. Relatively few homes contained books, and few books were written for or made available to the young. Newspapers were comparatively expensive and were more often read in clubs than at home. Most lending libraries that did exist charged fees, and did not cater for children. There were no supermarkets, television, or junk mail. The new postage stamps were dear and letters uncommon in most families. Christmas and birthday cards were still to come. Consequently few young children had much exposure to print outside school. They went to school to learn to read, and the school readers were what they read. Before the nineteenth century the proportion of readers in the population was even smaller. Written language was even more restricted in its distribution and the chances of anyone acquiring written language through incidental exposure were insignificant.

The situation now is very different. In our society everyone, regardless of age or social class, is bombarded with written language. Our food and drink comes in packages with printed messages. A trip to the supermarket is a very meaningful reading lesson, supported by floods of advertising on television and through the letterbox. Junk mail, with its combination of words with pictures of familiar objects, is an ideal aid to decoding written language. In addition to junk mail we have real mail—bills and official notices, letters and greetings cards. Nearly every home contains newspapers and magazines, and most contain books. There are thousands of books for preschoolers, and lending libraries are free. The few households that contain little printed matter generally have television sets. Television projects a lot of written language, not just in deliberately educational programs such as Sesame Street, but in commercials, titles, credits, and subtitles. Commercials and titles especially are repetitive, accompanied by speech, and designed for quick recognition.

For the first time in human history large numbers of children are looking at sufficient visual language to be able to catch it, to learn to decode written language through everyday exposure to print. Babies are seeing written language from their cradles (or at least from their baby buggies). Most of them, certainly, do not see as much written language as they hear spoken language. The question is—are they seeing enough written language in meaningful situations (such as on babyfood jars) to crack the code? At what age will they have seen enough written language to recognize at least some words?

Presumably, given the necessary equipment and practice time, they could also learn to reproduce this language without formal teaching. Few parents give babies writing implements, for obvious reasons, and so first attempts at replication are likely to be delayed in comparison to first attempts at replicating spoken or signed languages, for which the only equipment required is the infant's own body. Consequently, the commencement of formal education is likely to occur at around the same time as the child first has the opportunity to start to reproduce written language, so it will be hard to separate "caught" from "taught" writing skills, at least until keyboards, which require less coordination and are less "dangerous" than pens or pencils, percolate into the nursery.

READING AND WRITING

Written language may have input advantages over speech, but it has output disadvantages. The print babies see is generally ready-made. Most of the surrounding written language is not produced by the people to whom the babies are closest, and this may reduce its interest and affect the babies' motivation to decode it and to reproduce it. They do not watch the production process in the same way as they see and hear the production process when their parents talk to them (or sign to them), so there is nothing to mimic. Indeed, as said above, mimicking the production of written language (as opposed to sign) requires tools—pen and paper—not usually put into the hands of infants.

Writing is an act that requires considerable physical skill. The neuromuscular coordination required to write may not be as great as that required to speak, but it is nonetheless considerable, and the opportunities for practice are fewer.[5] Writing makes substantial demands on motor memory and motor planning. These are often problem areas for people with severe speech impairments, who may have as much difficulty with handwriting (and manual sign) as they do with speech.[6]

Babies understand more words than they can say, and older children and adults with severe speech impairments usually understand *much* more than they can say.[7] Similarly, 6-year-olds can usually read more than they can write, and older children and adults with writing impairments are likely to be able to read much more than they can write. Fortunately there are strategies for producing written language that do not involve handwriting—typing, pointing to letters on alphabet boards, moving magnetic letters or letter blocks (like a typesetter)—all these circumvent motor planning problems. For individuals with more severe physical problems a large range of spelling strategies that require no hand skills is available. Many individuals who can neither speak nor write have successfully undertaken college education using alternative strategies for producing written language. In the same way that the decoding of print can be disassociated from the ability to read aloud, the ability to spell can be disassociated from the ability to write.

READING AND PEOPLE WITH SEVERE COMMUNICATION IMPAIRMENTS

People with severe expressive problems may have relatively minor or nonexistent input problems. It is vitally important to separate the two. If we judge what goes in, and what goes on inside, by what comes out, we are likely to underestimate the potential of people with expressive problems. If we overlook their potential to acquire literacy skills, we are denying them the most powerful alternative to speech available in our society.

Speech and comprehension, spelling and reading, are dependent on different pathways and processes. Just as we understand more words than we ourselves use in everyday speech there can be a discrepancy between the words we are able to read and the words we can spell.

Input/Internal Processes	*Output Processes*
Hearing/Comprehension	Speech
Seeing/Reading	Spelling (writing or typing)

If there is difficulty with the output processes (speech disturbance, inability to coordinate hands for writing) it is hard to tell how well the input processes are working just by listening to or looking at what a person is doing. To establish how much spoken or written language a person can understand it is necessary to use assessments and equipment that circumvent any expressive problems.

The myths about literacy that have dominated our approaches to reading have often led us to overlook the potential of people with disabilities to acquire and use literacy skills. Many individuals with severe communication impairments who have been labeled as intellectually impaired have acquired reading skills from exposure. Their families and teachers are in most cases unaware of their skills because their inability to speak or write has prevented them from showing anyone that they can understand written language. Some individuals have behaviors (such as always buying certain magazines, or sitting down with a newspaper for half an hour every day, or taking a book to bed every night) that in people without disabilities would certainly have been viewed as associated with reading. Because their families and teachers have absorbed all the myths about literacy, because they do not expect these people to have those skills, they often overlook this evidence.

"Paul" has Down syndrome. His mother thought it was so sweet the way Paul imitated his sisters by sitting and pretending to read for an hour when he came home from school each day. He chose age-appropriate books, held them the right way up, turned the pages one-by-one, moved his eyes from left to right and down the page[8], but he couldn't speak well enough to say what he had read and he could scarcely write at all so his family presumed he wasn't understanding the words on the page. At the age of 12, Paul was given a chance to type for the first time. He revealed good reading comprehension, an excellent vocabulary, and appalling spelling!

To ensure that individuals with disabilities have the opportunity to acquire literacy skills, it is important that they have the same exposure to print as their nondisabled peers. All children should be read to, with the book held in a position where they can see the pictures and the print. Children whose physical impairments prevent them from holding books or turning pages need recipe book stands or pageturners in order to be able to look at books. Children who tear books can be given cheap books, magazines, or junk mail to look at until they are able to care for books.[8] The important thing is to ensure that every child, especially every child with severe communication impairments, has as much exposure to written language as possible. It can do no harm, and may do significant good.

Older children or adults with severe disabilities may have some acquired literacy skills regardless of whether they have had access to formal education. Observers may see incidents or behavior that indicate an interest in or understanding of written language. Maria always looks at the TV guide before she switches on the television, Liz went to the bookshelves and got the book her father had asked for, Tony puts on whatever song the staff ask for even though none of the records have covers, and Dean goes up to the notice board every time a new notice goes up.

Assessment of literacy skills in people who cannot talk or write requires patience and creativity. The materials used must be motivating and age appropriate. Multiple choice activities such as selecting the appropriate written word to complete a sentence, choosing the cartoon that best matches a caption, or picking the correct written answer to general knowledge questions can be varied to suit different age groups and interests. Individuals with hand function impairments may need to be taught selection strategies such as finger or eye pointing in order to be able to make meaningful responses to multiple choice questions. The absence of effective selection skills should not be taken as indicating anything about the person's actual or potential literacy skills.

Obviously there will be individuals who do not demonstrate literacy skills on initial assessment. Some may have sensory impairments that have affected their ability to pick up on written and/or spoken language without special aids or teaching strategies. Some will have lacked the incidental exposure necessary to acquire written language without formal teaching (this is most likely to apply to people who have spent prolonged time in residential care and individuals whose caregivers are not literate or who do not speak the same language as the community at large). Some people may have had incidental exposure but not have taken any interest in written language, perhaps because they saw it as having no relevance to them. All of these people are likely to benefit from exposure to meaningful written language, and all are candidates for literacy programs.

The importance of literacy skills to people with severe communication impairments cannot be overstated. Signing can certainly provide a powerful alternative to speech, but it is effective only for individuals with unimpaired handskills who live in signing communities. Most individuals with severe communication impairments have poor handskills and live among nonsigners. The only communication strategy that offers these people access to an unrestricted vocabulary is spelling. Without spelling skills the individual with severe communication impairments is restricted to using picture, sign, or word displays that have a limited vocabulary selected by caregivers, teachers, or therapists, and reflecting their views of what the person wants to say and how they should say it. Even poor spelling or the ability to identify initial letters will significantly expand a communication aid user's vocabulary options. Tina points to the symbol for "animal" and the letter "d"—Tina could be talking about dogs, donkeys, ducks, or dolphins. While her communication partner will have to ask yes/no questions to establish which animal Tina is referring to, this is more empowering than having either only a small number of specific animal symbols available or having to play 20 questions with the whole of the animal kingdom.

Spelling is the only strategy that allows individuals with severe communication impairments to communicate about whatever they choose in the words they choose.

Despite everyone's best efforts there will still be some individuals with severe communication impairments for whom the acquisition of literacy skills is difficult or impossible. Fortunately there are a number of nonspeech communication options such as picture and symbol displays that do not require reading or spelling available for this group. These options are also appropriate for use by young children and individuals in the process of acquiring spelling skills. As lack of speech should not be confused with inability to read, neither should inability to read be confused with inability to communicate Individuals who cannot spell may still need facilitation in order to point accurately to pictures or symbols.

ENDNOTES

[1] An engrossing account of the development of deaf education is given in *Seeing Voices* by Oliver Sacks (Picador, London, 1989).

[2] This was not always the case. It was recorded, correctly or not, that St. Augustine was the first European who could read without moving his lips. The written European languages were developed as ways of recording spoken languages and they were taught as a representation of spoken language whose form varied with the pronunciation and conventions used by the writer. Instead of decoding visual language directly most readers translated text into aural language and decoded that. Direct decoding of written language, without intervening translation to the aural mode, was given impetus by the development of the printing press and the dictionary, which combined to give written language a standard presentation unaffected by changes in spoken language.

[3] That is not to say that there will not be some people for whom reading is difficult or impossible. There will be a small percentage of people who have word blindness in the same way as there will be a small percentage of people who have word deafness.

[4] Of course, this theory of language learning raises questions about what we mean when we say a language is "taught." It may be that a language teacher's role is merely to set up a situation in which the language can be caught—it may be that attempts to teach language (any language) in the way that second languages were typically taught in my youth, largely by rote learning, were in fact counterproductive, that they delayed acquisition of the inner structure of the language by breaking the language up into externally imposed categories such as irregular verbs. If humans have, as appears to be the case, a knack for acquiring language in infancy,

then it is the acquisition strategies that work so effectively for infants that we should be capitalizing on in teaching all languages, at least for as long as they are effective. (There is evidence that we lose the wonderful language acquisition skills of infancy in later childhood.) While most of us did learn some French, German, or whatever language we were taught in school, we may have done so despite rather than because of the teaching strategies used. The teachers provided us with a little exposure to the language, so we learnt a little of the language. If we were keen students we also learned what ever our teachers taught us. To this day I can decline "voco," down to and including the pluperfect subjunctive passive. Sadly I still cannot decode a sentence of Virgil without a crib. Latin is a dead language, and all I picked up was its bones.

5 As all the equipment for speech is built in, it is automatic for babies to try and use it, part of the developmental program they are born with. As the equipment for written language is not built in, there is no such automatic attempt to try to write.

6 Many people who cannot write can type, because typing uses visual rather than motor memory. Of course, they may still have problems with spelling, and may still be able to decode written language better than they can spell it, in the same way as many people without disabilities can read words easily that they find difficult to spell.

7 And when we are in a non-English speaking country we are likely to understand more than we can say.

8 Some individuals who do not treat written material appropriately may still have reading skills—Don tore books and magazines because he found it hard to turn the pages, Lyn could not slow down enough to read a whole page, but both had excellent comprehension skills and went on to do well at high school.

5

Do's and Don'ts for Receivers of Nonspeech Communication

＋＋ ⊫◊⊨ ＋＋

- *Do be patient*
We can talk at 150 words per minute; many communication aid users cannot communicate at 150 words an hour.

- *Do be confident*
Any nervousness or doubts on your part will certainly be transmitted to the aid user, often with disastrous effects on their confidence.

- *Do monitor your own communication*
Are you talking down to the aid user? Do you raise your voice when you talk to someone who cannot speak? Does your interaction consist largely of orders and prohibitions?

- *Do use the right method*
Find out exactly how the user accesses the communication aid and how it should be positioned, and be consistent. If possible, observe someone who is communicating fluently with the aid user and ask them to observe your early attempts. Achieve success in small things before aiming for in-depth discussion.

- *Do provide appropriate feedback*
In the early stages of communication it often helps the user if the receiver says each letter or symbol aloud as it is indicated, and repeats the utterance to date at the end of each word. Further on, the user will probably prefer it if their partner does not say the utterance aloud until it is completed (and then only if it is not private).

• *Do pay attention*
It is as important for the aid user to feel that you are interested as it is for you to feel the person you are talking to is listening. If the aid user is inexperienced, monitor the output, and warn the user if you cannot understand it, so that corrections can be made before there is an irretrievable communication breakdown.

• *Do offer word or sentence completions*
Remember, the purpose of aid use is communication, not a spelling test. Most aid users will appreciate it if you comple___ words wh___ the mean___ is obv___. You can see why this would be helpf___. But do be careful not to jump in too early and put words into the user's mouth.

• *Do look out for abbreviations*
Many aid users use shorthand to speed communication, such as RUOK ("are you ok?"). Some use unconventional or phonetic spelling such as NE for "any." Interpretation is a lot easier if the user is encouraged to put spaces between words—at least then you know where one "word" finishes and the next starts.

• *Do clarify meaning*
Many users produce telegraphic utterances (as I am sure I would in their place). A user whose communication system only has a limited vocabulary obviously has no choice but to make approximations. In these cases it is necessary to play 20 questions to ascertain the user's exact meaning. Make it a practice to ask the user if you've got it right at the end of each utterance—if the aid does not produce written output it is very easy for the receiver to muddle a sequence of words or symbols. The aid user is also as prone to second thoughts and confusion as the rest of us, but has little chance to have a second go if we don't check.

• *Do respond appropriately*
It is easy to get so involved in the process that one forgets that the user wants a response. You may need to ensure tactfully that others around the user also respond. It is very discouraging for someone to expend a great deal of effort to spell "Hi! How are you?" only to be ignored.

• *Do empower the aid user*
Arrange for the aid user to be able to make *real* choices (not just to "choose" to have lunch when it's lunch time anyway!). Act on the

aid user's requests and comments whenever possible, and explain and apologize if it is not possible.

• *Do encourage aid use everywhere*
Our communication is not restricted to particular times and places. Neither should an aid user's be restricted. Inconvenience is not a good reason to refuse communication. If the situation is really difficult, for example, if the bus is waiting, ask if the communication is urgent (after all, the person may have mislaid something important or need the toilet). If the communication is not urgent, fix another time for a chat *and stick to it.* If there is a practical problem, such as not being able to use an electronic aid in the swimming pool, try and find a practical solution (e.g., a Perspex communication board).

• *Do encourage the expression of feelings*
Many aid users have used their aids only to make choices or to answer basic questions. They need encouragement to enter into longer conversations and to reveal more of themselves.

• *Do respect confidentiality*
If an aid user says something clearly not designed for public consumption, resist the temptation to pass it on, no matter how interesting or amusing it is. Remember, adults (and children) have the right not to have everything they say reported to their parents. If the user's aid produces written output make sure the tape is disposed of carefully unless it was produced as part of a specific educational program or you have the user's permission to keep it.

• *Do keep up your side of the conversation*
Volunteer your opinions. Tell the aid user what you have been doing. It is slow and tiring for the user to ask questions and not unusual for the user to not receive an answer. The aid user is always asked to give information in response to your questions, and expects you to respond in turn

• *Do recognize the effort and frustration involved*
Using a communication aid to give a message is far more laborious, and far more likely to be misunderstood, than giving the same message in speech. Consequently, it is important that unnecessary or repetitive questions are avoided, such as asking someone what they had for lunch when you just fed them.

- *Do avoid testing*

Many aid users have very negative attitudes toward questions they perceive as testing and will often deliberately give wrong answers. Testing should be kept to appropriate situations, such as the class-room. After all, we are not required to establish our competence every time we open our mouths. If we were, we might not talk very much. The aid user who feels that every interaction is a test is likely to become resistant to the whole idea of communication. A no-fail question such as "What color do you like best, blue, or pink?" is more likely to get a response than a question such as "What color is the sky?"

- *Do take the blame for failure*

If the communication attempt is unsuccessful, accept responsibility. After all, you do not have the excuse of having a communication impairment! A statement such as "I'm sorry. I'm not at my best today. Let's have another go tomorrow" helps the aid user to main-tain confidence.

- *Don't be negative!*

6

Getting Physical—Posture and Upper Limb Functioning

⊷ ⥅⥈ ⊶

Pointing accurately to a small target such as a letter on a keyboard is a very complex task that most of us take for granted. Think of what is involved. First you localize the target, usually by looking at it. Then your brain computes where you are in space, where the target is in space, and the strength and direction of movement needed to hit it. At the same time it instructs your index finger to point, your other fingers to flex, and your arm to extend. If either you or the target is moving, the distance and direction have to be recomputed and adjustments to your movements made after you have started to point.

Top tennis players have brains that are very good at carrying out these recomputations and muscles trained to act at speed. Most of us cannot return Pete Sampras's serves but may still be able to catch a Frisbee. Those of us who cannot catch Frisbees and have difficulty coordinating our movements need to reduce the complexity of the tasks we face as well as work on specific skills.

Accurate pointing is more difficult if either the person pointing or the target is moving, so the easiest way to simplify the task is to make sure that both the person and the target are stable. The first element in providing a stable base from which to move is to provide appropriate seating. The second element is to develop trunk and shoulder control so that the body is maintained in an upright position with the shoulder girdle horizontal and not subject to unpredictable movements. In facilitated communication proximal stability is sometimes increased by the application of firm pressure at the shoulder, but the long-term aim is for each individual to increase his or her own stability so external pressure is unnecessary. Finally,

47

accurate pointing at a small target or use of a keyboard requires the ability to use one finger in isolation.

GIVE ME A SEAT—I HAVE SOMETHING TO SAY

Stable, functional, and comfortable seating is essential for carrying out everyday tasks such as using a knife and fork and writing or typing. Physical performance is intimately associated with good seating. Poor posture further restricts the ability of people with physical limitations to do tasks and to observe their environment, and may lead to painful physical deformities or retard their overall development. Many individuals who need to use communication aids have significantly impaired hand function that will be further diminished by inappropriate seating.

Children who have not learned or experienced postural stability may have to apply a continuous conscious effort to sitting. Unless they have appropriate postural support their ability to concentrate on tasks such as school work and communication can be severely impaired. With conditions such as cerebral palsy there is also a need to encourage maximum function by inhibiting undesirable movement patterns and reflexes

General Principles of Seating Provision

An appropriate chair will have the following characteristics:

1. Provide stable postural support.This has particular relevance for users of microcomputer systems and/or communication aids, who must have sufficient support and control of their head, trunk, and limbs to enable them to see a display screen and use a keyboard or switches.
2. Allow the person access to a stable working surface (a wheelchair tray or a table) of appropriate height.

Firm Base of Support

The most important aspect of seating is a FIRM BASE OF SUPPORT. Without this any person's hand use is severely impaired. An upright chair of appropriate size that has any padding firmly attached to a rigid seat is most suitable for people using their hands.

The pelvis provides the base of support for the upper body. If the pelvis is not positioned firmly and symmetrically it will not provide the support necessary for arm movements and may contribute to spinal deformity.

People with lateral instability may be helped by using a chair with a narrow seat and high arms. Care should be taken to ensure that the chair has a wide enough base to prevent it from tipping if the person leans to one side. People who have difficulty maintaining hip flexion, and who tend to slide forward on the seat can be helped by covering the seat with high-friction fabric, such as the webbing that is used to prevent rugs and bath mats from slipping. This fabric may also be used on the work surface to prevent the communication aid from sliding away.

Seating for People with Low Muscle Tone

People with low muscle tone find it harder to hold up their bodies and arms against gravity. Most people with Down syndrome have low muscle tone, as do many other people with developmental disabilities. Having chairs and tables of a suitable height is especially important and particular attention needs to be paid to those peolple who are shorter than average. A firm base of support will be provided if the following points are followed:

1. The ankles, knees, and hips should be at right angles. The feet should be flat on the floor or a firm surface. If the seat is too high the chair legs should be cut to the correct length or a stable footrest provided. The rungs of a chair do not provide an adequate support for the feet. If the seat is too low blocks under the chair legs may be used to raise it. If this is not possible a firm cushion can be used (several posture cushions are available commercially). If posture cushions (Figure 6.1) are to be used it is essential that they are firmly secured to the chair and do not slip. The best solution is gluing. It is important that the cushion is firm and not too soft, as softness will promote a slumping.
2. The length of the seat should be long enough to give adequate support to the thighs.
3. The person should be encouraged to sit well back in the chair, not perch on the edge of the seat (Figure 6.2).

People with low tone have their ability to use their hands affected by the height of the work surface or table. If this is too high they

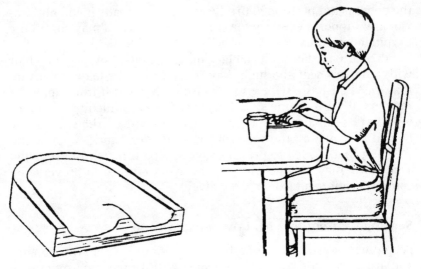

Figure 6.1. Posture cushion (Thera-peutic Pillow International).

Figure 6.2. Use of posture cushion to adjust height and angle of seat.

will tire quickly. Armrests on a chair can provide support for elbows and forearms, but may be cumbersome. If armrests prevent the person from drawing his or her chair close to the table this will result in undue strain and lead to early fatigue.

Tables should be high enough for people to be able to sit close with feet underneath and forearms resting on the table surface. The correct height of the table depends on the task to be undertaken. For writing the forearms should be able to rest comfortably on the table, but for keyboard work the table should be lower, just above the thighs. Alternatively, it may be best for the person to work with the keyboard or communication aid on his or her lap. The ideal way to accommodate the work surface requirements of groups of people who are of different heights and use different chairs is to use adjustable height tables. The most suitable of these allows the angle as well as the height of the table to be adjusted and have bases that are horseshoe shaped, thus providing unobstructed space for the chair to be wheeled into the open end.

Height adjusters and cushions may be the only way to modify the molded plastic chairs with metal legs unfortunately favored in many schools.

A Quick Checklist for Good Seating

The checklist is useful for ensuring that a person is sitting comfortably and is ready for work. Is the person sitting

1. well back in the chair with spine as close as possible to the middle of the chair back?
2. with feet on a firm base either on floor or footplates with toes pointing to front?
3. with knees in line with hips?
4. with thighs adequately supported—that is, is the seat long enough, ending two fingers short of the back of the knees?
5. with arm rests of the right height, so that the shoulders are not drooping or hunched?
6. with the head facing the task to be undertaken and not the floor or ceiling?
7. with the work surface at the correct height in relation to the seat and to the task to be undertaken?
8. comfortably?

All the answers need to be in the affirmative to optimize hand function.

SHOULDER GIRDLE ACTIVITIES

The muscles of the shoulder, upper body, and arms must be strong to permit good hand function. The muscles of the upper body act as stabilizers so that the hands can perform tasks accurately and effectively. If these muscles are weak a person will find it hard to sustain an activity such as using a keyboard because he will be unable to maintain his hands in the correct position.

Paul has Down syndrome and low muscle tone. Because of this he hasn't played much sport. Correspondingly, his low muscle tone was complicated by low muscle strength—he hadn't been using his arm and shoulder muscles as much as other children, so they were weaker. When his family realized the problem they started going to the local pool regularly, where Paul swam laps. Also, Paul's father put up a basketball hoop on the garage and Paul spent half-an-hour each evening happily shooting baskets when he came home from school. Not only did Paul's typing improve; he developed skills that helped him to participate successfully in group sporting activities at school.

An important factor in developing and maintaining muscle strength is participation—participation in all those activities of daily life that are routine for children and adults without disabilities, activities such as carrying shopping, housework, and gardening, as well as swimming and ball games. Following is a short list of activities that will strengthen the arm and shoulder muscle groups— obviously there are many others.

- volleyball
- basketball/netball—shooting goals
- swimming
- tug-of-war
- washing the floor on hands and knees with a cloth
- using a squeeze mop
- using a broom, especially outdoors
- raking leaves
- washing windows and mirrors, especially above shoulder height
- putting things on high shelves
- scrubbing the bath or the shower recess
- digging in the garden
- doing pushups
- hanging out the washing or bringing it in (winding the line up high)
- painting large surfaces such as fences or walls
- climbing—gym ladders, monkey bars, climbing frames, or ropes
- squeezing oranges or lemons
- cleaning the cobwebs from the ceiling
- changing light bulbs
- rowing (or using rowing machines)
- weight lifting (or wearing wrist weights while doing other activities)
- upper-body aerobics
- mowing the lawn with a hand mower
- pushing prams or shopping carts
- fruit picking

If the person has a history of arthritis, fractures, contractures, dislocations, or other painful hand or arm problems, do consult a therapist before undertaking any activities.

People with motor-planning problems may need initial assistance in developing the movement patterns necessary to succeed at specific activities. For example, Don positioned himself behind Tom and placed his hands over Tom's so he could help Tom catch and throw a basketball. He reduced his input as Tom's skills improved.

IMPROVING FINGER-POINTING SKILLS

Despite what our mothers told us, it's not always rude to point. Pointing is a very useful skill and is especially important for people with severe speech impairments, as it offers a powerful means of augmenting their speech. An infant may point at the toy they want, an older child may point at symbols on a communication board, a teenager may type.

For effective finger pointing you need to be able to extend one finger, usually the index finger, of the preferred hand while keeping back the other fingers. You also need to have the eye-hand coordination to line up the finger and the target.

Problems

The main problems we have seen with finger-pointing and some remedies are:

DIFFICULTY ISOLATING ONE FINGER

That is, difficulty extending one finger while keeping the others back. The student should be encouraged to do exercises using only one finger. It may be necessary to hold the other fingers back at first until the isolation becomes habitual. Some children wear an old sock with a small hole cut in it pulled down over the dominant hand and held at the wrist with a tie, so that only the index finger can extend through the hole. This should be used only while using a communication aid or doing pointing exercises. If index finger isolation shows no improvement after a few weeks of exercises, seek further advice from an occupational therapist.

WEAKNESS

That is, there is difficulty stiffening the index finger and applying pressure. Preference should be given to finger exercises requiring pressure, and every effort made to ensure that the finger remains straight when pressing. Splints are used as a last resort in the rare instances where the exercises do not produce sufficient improvement. We do not encourage the early use of splints or the provision of finger support by facilitators because these strategies are unlikely to result in the strengthening of the finger muscles and therefore entail continued dependency on splinting or facilitation.

WOBBLE

That is, the finger moves from side to side, resulting in uncertainty as to the selection wanted or, if a keyboard is being used, producing typing errors. As for weakness, preference should be given to exercises involving pressure. The stability of the wrist should be assessed as well as the finger. Often the problem with the finger is produced or made worse by the wrist's lateral instability. If this is the case, exercises to strengthen and balance the arm muscles will also be needed.

POOR EYE-HAND COORDINATION

That is, pointing without looking or failing to keep the eyes on the target, resulting in incorrect selections. Any activities involving selection from a set of items may be used for eye-hand coordination practice. Choose materials that are as interesting and age appropriate as possible—say picture books and insert puzzles for a preschooler, jigsaws for a primary student, pop stars and footballers for a teenager. The activities are meant to be fun, not a test. The sole aim is to ensure that when students point they are looking at where they are pointing. It does not matter if the pointing is coactive at the start, as long as the students keep their eyes on the target.

Many individuals have more than one of these problems. Sometimes this means they need to do several kinds of activities to remedy all their difficulties, sometimes it is possible to find an activity that addresses more than one problem. For example, the Touch and Tell, made by Texas Instruments, is a toy with bright picture overlays that speaks when the overlay is pressed. It requires firm pressure to operate it, so it can be used to address weakness and wobble problems as well as provide a good stimulus for eye-hand coordination training.

Some activities require more supervision than others. Care should be taken at the start of all activities to ensure that the movements are being performed correctly—it is, unfortunately, perfectly possible to operate a Touch and Tell with the whole fist without looking at all, but of course no improvement in finger pointing will result. Supervised exercises for 5 or 10 minutes a day usually produces rapid improvement in index finger isolation and strength.

Sometimes caregivers and teachers feel it is easier to give a student a splint or a pointer than do exercises to compensate for index finger isolation and weakness problems. While it is quicker initially, consider the time needed to make and hunt for pointers/splints in the future. If we can improve the students' own hands, we are giving them skills they will have for the rest of their lives. We think it is possible to develop independent index finger pointing skills in almost all individuals with developmental disabilities who do not have severe cerebral palsy or hand deformities.

As students improve their pointing skills it is important to encourage increased independence. Students can be encouraged to point independently to desired foods, drinks or activities when appropriate. The support offered to students using facilitated communication should be reduced as their finger pointing improves. Students who can isolate their index fingers do not require their hands held, though they may still require wrist support to counteract other problems, such as tremor.

Following is a short list of activities that can be used to encourage finger isolation and to strengthen the index finger. All may be done coactively if necessary. Do make sure the student looks at what he or she is doing.

- Poking holes in balls of clay, plasticine, or PlaDoh.
- Poking holes in plastic wrap stretched over a bowl.
- Pushing finger into a balloon. (Watch out!)
- Drawing *with the tip of one finger* in fingerpaint or shaving cream on table or mirror.
- Using toys with push buttons or dials (e.g., toy phones).
- Using educational toys that require pressure to make a selection, e.g., Touch and Tell.
- Pushing holes in soil to plant seeds.
- Pointing to pictures or parts of pictures.
- Pointing to pieces from insert board or jigsaw puzzle to show you what goes where.
- Playing picture lotto, dominoes, and card games where matching items can be indicated by pointing.
- Playing keyboard toys or musical instruments—again, played with only one finger.
- Making collage pictures by pointing to item wanted and then to the place on the paper where it should be pasted.
- Tracing patterns and shapes in wet sand.

Remember to make use of everyday situations (flushing the toilet, turning lights on and off, pressing pedestrian buttons, selecting a TV channel, operating a cassette player, dialing the phone, operating household equipment, etc.) to develop index finger skills. These not only develop pointing skills, they are motivating and necessary activities in their own right.

7

Reducing Support—Increasing Independence

＋ ＝◆＝ ＋

Facilitated communication training is used with people with severe communication impairments who are not yet able to access a communication aid independently but for whom independent direct access using their hands is a realistic and desirable goal. It is part of a process and not an end in itself.

Communication aid users may initially need physical assistance from their communication partners while they develop specific skills such as index finger isolation. As the aid users' skills increase the amount of physical assistance they receive should diminish. The ultimate aim is for the users to access their communication aids with no physical contact from their communication partners.

This aim is not always achieved. There will be some people who commence facilitated communication training but find that even after considerable training, independent aid access is still impossible, or at least still so slow and arduous so as to severely limit their communication. These people need their communication strategies reviewed. They may change to indirect access (using a scanning system), they may continue with direct access in another modality (eye-pointing, for instance), or they may elect to remain facilitated, perhaps being independent in some situations and not others.[1] However, this group is a minority and the presumption when starting facilitated communication training should be that the user will eventually move on to independent access.

To ensure that users do not become overly dependent on their facilitators it is important that all facilitators are aware from the start that independence is the goal. It is also important that attempts are made to fade support as soon as a person starts to use a communication aid successfully with facilitation.

The first step in reducing dependency is for all communication partners to give the minimum support required for communication to succeed. The second step is to ensure that the aid user communicates with as many different partners as possible. In order to successfully fade support it is necessary to know what problem or problems the individual had that needed facilitation in the first place.[2]

Some problems are remedied directly by the facilitation process. Eye-hand coordination problems, for example, usually improve quite rapidly if facilitators consistently refuse to allow aid users to make a selection unless they are looking at their aids. In this case it is easy for facilitators to monitor improvement in users. Facilitators record the number of times each aid user has to be reminded to bring his or her eyes back to the task in a 5-minute period. As soon as it is routine for a user to get through 5 minutes without a reminder physical contact should be withdrawn as quickly as is possible without the aid user regressing. Spoken prompts may initially be needed as a substitute.

Other problems may require other therapy in addition to the communication sessions themselves, or may require the aid user to learn special strategies. Low muscle tone and weak fingers require specific exercise routines or adaptations in daily activities to build up muscle strength. Some aid users who have difficulty isolating an index finger may be able to type without hand support when holding a pen in the palm of the typing hand with their other fingers. People who have difficulties with perseveration may be helped by learning to hit a dot on the table after typing each letter.[3]

Other factors may also affect independence. Some people have variable muscle tone, and may be able to type independently one day but not the next. Some people are independent in familiar surroundings with familiar people, but out in public become nervous and seek support. It is important to provide the temporary support needed in these situations. Not only does the individual have a right to communicate, the nervousness is only going to be cured by an increase in confidence, and this is unlikely to occur if the person experiences communication failure or frustration when out in public.

Environment is an important factor in independence. A person with a tremor is not going to be helped by sitting on a chair that won't let their feet reach the floor. A person with low muscle tone is far more likely to be independent if the communication aid is positioned as low as possible, to minimize lifting against gravity. A person who is visually distractible will require fewer prompts to keep his or her eyes on task if facing a wall rather than a window looking on to a busy corridor.

There is a continuum in the provision of facilitation, running roughly through the stages listed below. Some of these stages are illustrated in Figures 7.1a–7.1h.

1. hand molding
2. rod (user holds rod while facilitator holds other end)
3. wrist support
4. forearm support
5. sleeve or elbow support
6. upper arm pressure
7. shoulder pressure
8. shoulder touch
9. physical contact with another part of the user's body[4]
10. independent access

Each person starting facilitated communication training needs a different level of support. It is important that everyone working with an individual is made aware of his or her particular support needs, and that no one provides more support than the minimum required. Where there are a number of aid users requiring facilitation it is understandably common for staff to adopt a lowest common denominator approach, all users being offered the level of facilitation required by the most dependent because that is guaranteed to succeed with everyone. Such an approach will almost guarantee continued dependence. If fading is to succeed it has to be individualized, has to be applied consistently, and has to start from each individual's baseline level of support.

Dependency may be related to aid and position. Many people with low muscle tone are initially more independent standing up, when they don't have to raise their arms against gravity. Such people may be independent using devices with small keyboards (such as the Canon Communicator) but still require some support when using a larger keyboard on a computer or typewriter. Some individuals can type without physical contact if their partners hold the communication aid low (and in this situation the partners' direct involvement may also provide emotional support and encouragement).

While independent communication is worthwhile even if it can be used only in certain situations, and while this situational inde-

Figure 7.1a. Hand molding to obtain index finger isolation.

Figure 7.1b. User holds a rod while facilitator holds the other end.

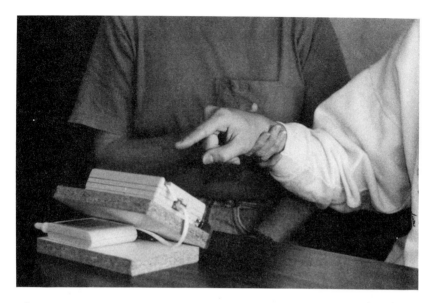

Figure 7.1c. Wrist support.

Figure 7.1d. Sleeve support.

Figure 7.1e. Elbow support.

Figure 7.1f. Upper arm pressure.

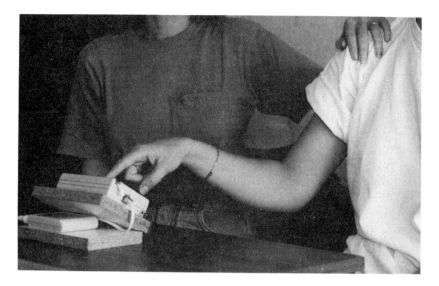

Figure 7.1g. Shoulder pressure.

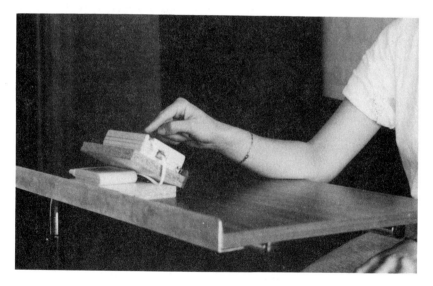

Figure 7.1h. Independent access with elbow supported on table.

pendence may be useful in validating a person's communication skills, the ultimate goal for all aid users should be the kind of independence that allows them to access all their communication aids in the most convenient manner. In the main this will be while the aids are on an appropriate height table. Correspondingly, during the period of fading support it is important to record at each stage the aid or aids that were used, the position of the aid, and the position of the individual—"shoulder touch when seated with Canon Communicator held low," for example—so that meaningful comparisons and evaluations of progress can be made. In order to monitor progress in increasing user independence it is essential to maintain complete records. The records will not only encourage continuance of the program but also identify problems or plateaus so that help can be sought.

The aim of every augmentative communication program is for the students involved to communicate with those around them as fluently and independently as possible. A reduction of support often initially results in a loss of speed and accuracy. It is important to ensure that students understand the aims of the program. They should never be made to feel that fading is a test, and that they have failed if it doesn't work out. Jane, for example, has low muscle tone. She types short sentences well with just a touch on her shoulder. However, she soon tires and starts making many mistakes. When this happens her facilitator offers her more support so she can finish what she wanted to say. Withdrawal of support should be a flexible process and aid users should feel secure in the knowledge that they will never be left unable to communicate.

Independent communication is the best kind, but even the worst kind of communication is much better than none at all. Independence is a valuable skill; communication is a basic human right.

Two model record forms are attached, one for the use of individual facilitators (Figure 7.2) and one for centers such as schools, adult centers, or residential units (Figure 7.3), which need to monitor the performance of aid users with numbers of facilitators. The individual form may either be filled in after every session or at a specific session once a week. The group form should be filled in at least once a month—some centers pass around a folder at their staff meetings containing a form for each person needing facilitation. The person in charge of the communication program should regularly review the updated forms to monitor trends so gaps or discrepancies can be investigated. For example, on the sample form several questions arise: If Joe is using his aid with just shoulder

Figure 7.2

Individual Facilitator's Client Record					
Client: Jane Smith			*Facilitator:* John Brown		
Date	Level of Support	Equipment Used	Position of Client	Position of Equipment	Task
3/2/92	3	Canon	Sitting	Table	X-word
10/2/92	3	"	"	"	Sentence completion
17/2/92	3	"	"	"	Captions
24/2/92	4	"	"	"	X-word
3/3/92	4	"	"	"	Conversation
10/3/92	3	Typewriter	"	"	Missing letters
17/3/92	4	Canon	"	"	Cloze exercise
24/3/92	6 (pressure)	"	"	Canon held low	Sentence completion
7/4/92	5	"	"	Table	Captions
14/4/92	5	"	"	"	Conversation

The level of support recorded should be the least support at which communication was successful during the session.

Legend: Amount of support required

1. Hand molding
2. Stick
3. Wrist support
4. Forearm support
– No opportunity

5. Sleeve or elbow support
6. Shoulder pressure/touch
7. Other body contact
8. No physical contact
X No success

Figure 7.3

_____ **Center: Client Record**						
Client: Joseph Blow						
Staff Member \ Date	9/8	3/9	25/10	29/11		
Kaye	3	3	6	6		
Annette	—	—	—	—		
Catherine	3	3	3	3		
Kerrie	—	—	—	—		
Janice	3	3	x	3		
Laurie	—	—	—	—		
Mark	—	—	—	—		
Linda	—	—	—	—		
Susan	—	3	x	3		
Debbie	—	—	—	—		
Hedda	5	5	—	—		
Don	—	—	—	—		
Veronica	—	—	—	—		

The level of support recorded should be the least support at which communication was successful.

Legend: Amount of support required

1. Hand molding
2. Stick
3. Wrist support
4. Forearm support
– No opportunity

5. Sleeve or elbow support
6. Shoulder pressure/touch
7. Other body contact
8. No physical contact
X No success

pressure from Kaye, why haven't other facilitators reduced their support? Why has Hedda had no opportunity to talk with Joe for 2 months? The number of Joe's communication partners appears to be static: What can be done to involve more staff?

ENDNOTES

[1] People who cannot access a large display or a keyboard without facilitation may be able to access a smaller number of items independently. This should be encouraged, both because it may lead to independence with the larger displays and because of the empowerment (and protection) it provides immediately. Being able to point to "yes" and "no" independently enables advisors to confirm or deny their facilitated communication. Being able to make clear, reliable selections from four items allows students to answer multiple choice questions.

[2] If there is any doubt, contact the agency or therapist who started the training program.

[3] Individual needs differ, and the appropriate strategies for each individual will vary. Again, the agency or therapist who set up the training program will be able to help.

[4] Sometimes for emotional reasons, sometimes to improve proprioception, and sometimes to maintain on-task behavior; some people with autism, in particular, seem to find it hard to maintain attention without some tangible reminder that they have "work" to do.

8

Word-Finding Problems

⚊ ⚌◈⚌ ⚊

WHAT IS A WORD-FINDING PROBLEM?

It is the inability to say or remember the word one wants. Sometimes the wrong word is said; sometimes nothing is said at all. The problem has been likened to going into the pantry in the dark to get a jar of honey and picking up a jar of marmalade instead or being unable to find a jar at all and coming out empty-handed.

We all experience this occasionally. In the supermarket queue you find yourself next to your child's teacher from last year. "Oh," you say, "How nice to see you, Miss Um-Er. Are you still teaching?" After you get home you remember that her name was Miss Gilbert.

You consider yourself reasonably intelligent, but could you remember the answer to questions if you were on a quiz show with a buzzer to push and an audience in front of you?

If you were asked, this minute, to name your neighbor two doors down, the chances are you would say "They're the . . . uh . . . um I'll think of it in a minute."

Can you imagine what it might be like to have this problem all the time?

WHY DOES IT OCCUR?

The use of language requires many functions of the brain to work together. Impaired development or damage of one or more functions or areas of the brain may interfere with the easy production of speech or language. The term expressive aphasia (or dysphasia) may be used in relation to someone with a word-finding problem.

It is thought that written and spoken language have different pathways, one of which may be stronger than the other.

One mode may be affected more than another, and a person may be able to recall words visually more easily than auditorily (or vice versa), and may write them more easily than say them. Words may be more easily recalled automatically, as in singing a familiar song, giving greetings, or swearing, than when the person makes a deliberate effort to remember, because different pathways are used in the brain for reflex or automatic speech than for planned speech.

It is important to note that difficulties with word-finding do not necessarily affect understanding or processing of spoken or written material.

WHICH WORDS ARE MOST DIFFICULT TO FIND?

Probably the most affected words are nouns, especially proper names. The problem is less noticeable on adjectives because it is easier to find a substitute. If you want to say a truck is "big" you can quickly alter your sentence to say the truck is "huge" or "gigantic" or "massive." It is not so easy to change if you are asked when you go swimming and you can't retrieve the word "Wednesday." Your choices may be to say nothing and be thought not to understand the question, or to say "Thursday" and hope it doesn't matter that you have got it wrong. Even "yes" and "no" may be a problem, with the person saying "no" when they mean "yes" or vice versa.

ARE THERE ANY COMMON ERROR PATTERNS?

Yes, several. These are the main ones:

1. *Associative*— calling an anchor a hook, for example, based on visual resemblance.
2. *Phonic*— saying "chair" when the wanted word is "chop."
3. *Categorical*— saying another word in the same category such as "pea" for "bean" or "Sydney" for "Melbourne."
4. *Functional*— saying "eat" for "fork" or "do hair" for "comb."
5. *Echoic*—like a cracked record, repeating oneself in an effort to find the correct word, or answering one question correctly and then giving the same answer to the next, different, question, or repeating the question instead of giving an answer.

HOW DO PEOPLE REACT TO
WORD-FINDING PROBLEMS?

THE SUFFERER

Often a person with a word-finding problem does not respond to
questions at all, for fear of saying the wrong thing, or says "I don't
know" when the true answer may be "I know, but I can't say it," or
gives an incorrect answer to please people rather than not give an
answer at all. They may say the wrong word and be too embar-
rassed to correct it or still be unable to find the right word even
though they know their answer has been wrong. If the problem is
severe they will be unable to explain their difficulty. We have
strategies like "I know the face, but I can't think of the name" and
"Give me a minute and I'll think of it" that the person with a severe
problem cannot use.

THE LISTENER

If the nature of the problem is not recognized the listener thinks the
person is uncooperative, deaf, or lacking in understanding.

Word-finding problems are not well understood, even by professionals. We all operate on the basis that a person's speech reflects
the person's thoughts. For the vast majority of us this is correct, and
it is hard to comprehend the difficulties of those for whom this is not
true. Having some, unpredictable speech may cause more problems
than having none. Sally's teachers punished her for being stubborn
every time she failed to answer a question. Of course, the tension
this caused made the problem worse. John had problems with "yes"
and "no." His teachers decided that the way to make him learn was
to act on his responses as though he meant them. John missed ice
cream and outings because he said "no" when he wanted to say
"yes." It was not surprising when he became a behavior problem.

WHAT TO DO

- Provide a supportive, uncritical environment. Reassure the
  person that you understand their difficulties.
- Give opportunities for correction. Say "Is that what you
  meant?" or "Are you sure?"
- Offer another method of communication. Some people can
  use spelling instead of speech. The different modality helps,

perhaps because it is slower and less automatic. The difficulty may still be present in typing but generally is less than in speech. If this is so, encourage the person not to talk while they are typing. Typing may be more successful than handwriting because people with word-finding problems may also have problems with motor memory and motor planning which impair their ability to write. The worksheet in Figure 8.1 illustrates this.

- Use strategies to assist speech. If you know what the word is that is wanted you may be able to give a clue. For instance, if the word is "chair" you might say "It's got four legs and you sit on it." You may be able to cue the correct word by saying "You sit on a . . ." or you may cue phonically, "You sit on a ch . . ." You may also cue by association, by saying "Table and. . . ." All these strategies would have helped Sally and John.
- If the person is getting very uptight, come back to it when more relaxed—it's not the end of the world.
- If the person just can't get something out, it may be a proper name—perhaps you could offer suggestions or alternatives.
- Remember that the person may want so badly to get out his words he may give any word at all if he can't find the right one. Give reassurance and an opportunity to correct.
- If the person can't get the next word when typing read back what has been typed already. Say "You've typed 'He sat on the . . .'—that's right, you know what it is."

Remember (teachers especially)—if someone has a word-finding problem, speech is not going to provide an appropriate means of assessing knowledge. Some children with relatively minor word-finding problems can read aloud accurately because the cue given by the written word enables them to overcome their difficulties. Those with more severe problems cannot, though their reading comprehension may be unaffected.

Written language may be less affected than speech. A child asked the capital of the Australia may say "Melbourne" but type "Canberra." Sometimes production of written language is as severely affected as speech production, in which case multiple choice assessment will provide the student's best chance of success. Linda could not say or write the capital of Victoria, but she could select "Melbourne" correctly from a list of the state capitals.

Understandably, lack of confidence is often a pervasive sec-

Figure 8.1. Comparison of spoken, written, and typed responses.

This worksheet was completed by a student using three modes—*speech*, handwriting, and `TYPING`. Her spoken replies reflect her marked word-finding problems, and her handwriting shows the effects of motor planning and motor memory problems. Her internal language is more sophisticated than she can display in either speech or writing. It is only when the motor demands of expression are reduced by using a typewriter that she can demonstrate this.

What Happened Next?

The baby pulled the cat's tail.	*Get hurt* THE CAT SCRATCHES THE BABY
The milk boiled over.	*Spilt everywhere* IT SPILT EVERYWHERE
The car went through a red light.	*Stop immediately* MAN COULDN'T STOP HE HAD BAD BRAKES
The policeman knocked on the door and called out:	*Shouting very loud* STOP MAKING SO MUCH NOISE DONT YOU KNOW ITS LATE
The dentist asked John: Put Your theeth out	*Want your teeth out* DO YOU WANT YOUR TEETH OUT
Last week Jane went to the zoo and saw some aimlas atthe Zoo	*Saw some animals at the zoo* SAW SOME ANIMALS AT THE ZOO
Tomorrow I would like to eat some food	*Eat some food* EAT SOME FOOD AT MCDONALDS

ondary problem for people with significant word-finding difficulties. Try and imagine what it would be like to be perpetually uncertain about what (if anything) would come out when you tried to talk. To counteract this it is important that those around the person are informed of the problem and that every effort is made to ensure each interaction finishes on a positive note.

People with word-finding problems should be given access to specialist help. Speech pathologists can advise on strategies that can help them to get their messages across. Options include cueing the person with the initial sound of a troublesome word (if you know what they are trying to say), providing a book of words or pictures for self cueing, or using an augmentative communication strategy such as writing or typing.

9

Assessment of People with Severe Communication Impairment

People with severe communication impairments are often given intellectual or academic assessments by psychologists or teachers who are unaware of the exact nature of their neuromotor impairments and the effect of these on the assessment process. Unfortunately many people with severe communication impairments have been denied the therapy they require, along with access to educational opportunities, because the results of inappropriate testing appear to show that they have such significant intellectual impairments that their ability to benefit from training would be restricted.

Accurate assessment of people with severe communication impairments is far from easy. There may be individuals for whom no valid assessment measure can be found. Even more commonly, individuals will be found who require special training or equipment before they can be assessed accurately. These individuals should be given access to these resources without prejudice. The term "unassessable" means just that, and should not be thought of as a synonym for profound intellectual impairment. We all have an obligation to every person we assess to ensure that our testing is fair, and that the tests we use do test what they purport to test—that is, that the vocabulary test is purely a test of vocabulary, not simultaneously a test of visual or hand skills.

SELECTION OF TEST MATERIALS OR STRATEGIES

Choosing an appropriate test or assessment strategy for people with severe communication impairments is not easy. As with all testing, the first step is to decide what you're testing and why. A standard IQ test is of very little use in ascertaining whether Joe will be able to live independently, and if that's what you want to know then the necessary information is more likely to come from completion of a skills inventory.

The measure used has to be appropriate for the person's age and disability. Developmental screening tests such as the Denver or Bayley, which are designed to screen infants without major impairments for signs of developmental delay, are sometimes used inappropriately with older people who have severe or multiple impairments, and their results are then wrongly interpreted as indicating mental age. A pediatrician used the Denver Developmental Scale to assess Anne McDonald, a quadriplegic, when she was 17 years old. She failed to reach for the plastic ring he dangled in front of her and he gave her a mental age of 6 months. In addition to overlooking her quadriplegia he had also overlooked the fact that normal teenagers do not grab at plastic rings.

Most importantly, it is necessary to separate the communication disability from tests of comprehension, knowledge, or cognitive processing. A regular reading test may effectively become a speech test if reading aloud is included for a student with a severe speech impairment. The aim is to find a way of assessing the desired skill that does not require responses that are difficult or impossible for the individual with severe communication impairments. In the case of reading, comprehension tests with multiple choice answers are often useful if the student has adequate pointing skills.

Oral Responses

Performance on tests requiring oral responses (such as the WAIS or WISC) is adversely affected by speech impairments and is likely to understate the person's true capacity. People who have unreliable speech due to word-finding problems, aphasia or dyspraxia have special difficulties here, in that the true nature of their impairments may not be recognized by the tester. A person with word-finding problems, or aphasia may say the wrong answer, often using a related word, despite knowing the correct answer. Not surprisingly, a person with such a problem may be unwilling to respond to questions at all, and this lack of response may be confused with stubbornness or ignorance, as may be the sporadic responses of a person with dyspraxia.

Some people with word-finding problems read aloud more fluently than they speak spontaneously, because the written word cues their speech. Others find the written word no help; they may understand it but are still unable to say it, and either say nothing or say inappropriate words.

Echolalia is a specific word-finding problem in which the sufferer repeats the last word or words their communication partner says. Correspondingly responses to questions are unreliable, and will depend on how the question is asked. An echolalic conversation might go, for example,

Q: Is the capital of Australia Canberra or Melbourne?
A: Melbourne.
Q: Is the capital of Australia Melbourne or Canberra?
A: Canberra.
Q: What is the capital? Do you know?
A: No (know!)

Pointing Responses

Nonspeech tests (such as Raven's Matrices and the Peabody Picture Vocabulary Test) and the performance items of tests like the WAIS require pointing or manipulative responses. Obviously these cannot be used with people who have severe physical impairments precluding hand use (at least not without significant adaptation of the test presentation). Unfortunately, many people with severe communication impairments who can use their hands for gross motor activities still have neuromotor impairments that affect their pointing abilities.

Nonspeech and multiple choice tests are reliable only if it has been ascertained that the person with severe communication impairments has the neuromotor skills needed to make controlled responses. If there is any doubt, or if an individual does badly on a performance test, an occupational therapy assessment should be sought. It is entirely possible for individuals who have acquired quite good daily living skills with careful teaching to have motor problems that will effect their performance on test items. In fact, the block design tests that are included in the performance scales of the WAIS and Stanford-Binet had their origin in tests for apraxia, a neuromotor disorder that is not uncommon in people with severe communication impairments. Obviously, if an individual performs badly on a block design test, this may be caused by apraxia as much as by any problems of understanding or reason-

ing. Only a neuromotor assessment will disclose where the difficulty lies.

In addition to requiring hand skills, nonspeech assessments also
have visual requirements that should be kept in mind when ascertaining whether a particular test is going to provide an appropriate
means of assessment for a particular individual. In addition to the
visual acuity or color discrimination required—the person must be
able to see well enough to distinguish clearly the items from which
the answer has to be chosen—all such tests require scanning skills.
The person being tested must look at each of the alternatives in
order to select the correct answer. A person who only sees half the
answers, either because of hemianopia or because of poor scanning
techniques, is obviously disadvantaged. Poor scanning techniques
are usually remediable, either permanently through training, or
temporarily, by taking steps to ensure that the person looks at each
alternative—for instance, each option could be lit up in turn.

Problems with initiation, impulsivity, perseveration, and eye-
hand coordination will also affect the reliability of pointing
responses, as will fatigue.

Unfortunately, even when every precaution has been taken
and the test has been administered fairly the fact remains that the
standardized nonspeech tests only give limited information, and do
not provide much guidance in planning an educational program.
Results on the Peabody Picture Vocabulary Test, in particular, are
likely to be affected by a person's previous environmental experiences and educational background.

Written or Typed Responses

Some people with severe communication impairments can write or
type, either independently or with facilitation. Potentially this provides a powerful means of assessment; however, similar reliability
checks need to be made as for spoken communication or pointing.

HANDWRITING

Handwriting needs to be automatic and reasonably effortless before
it is an appropriate means of response. A person who has to devote
an inordinate amount of attention just to getting letters on the page
is not going to be able to simultaneously monitor the content and
spelling of the output.

Spontaneous writing uses motor memory—we have to recall
the shapes of the letters or words wanted and reproduce them on

paper. Copy writing does not make the same demands on motor memory, and some individuals with severe communication impairments can copy though they cannot write without a model. These people may have speech problems such as word-finding difficulties that may also involve difficulties in recalling motor patterns.

Low muscle tone may also produce handwriting problems—the person starts well but does not have the endurance to maintain quality and clarity, and often spelling tapers off as they tire.

Writing problems such as these may have no connection with the individual's actual literacy level—like the better known speech impairments, they merely affect the ability to express this knowledge.

TYPING

Perseveration, impulsivity, and other fine motor problems may interfere with the provision of correct typed responses—the person may type the same word or letter again and again, or they may start to type the correct answer but be locked into an "automatic" stereotyped response. For example, when asked the capital of Queensland—Brisbane—Phil typed BREAD. When asked the present tense of "brought" he also typed BREAD. He typed BREAD, in fact, when asked any question to which the correct answer started with BR.

WRITTEN LANGUAGE

A word-finding problem may extend to written language. If this is so, the ability to answer questions (especially those involving names of people or things) is quite likely to be affected. This gives rise to the situation where even if the individual being tested "knows" the answer he is only able to retrieve the right words if given a cue—that is, he can only give correct answers to those questions where he is cued by the communication partner either saying the initial sound or by assisting or reinforcing his movement toward the initial letter on a keyboard. (This often leads to communication with facilitation being questioned because the person with the severe communication impairments only answers correctly those questions to which the facilitator knows the answer).

TESTS OF COMMUNICATION COMPETENCE

Tests of communication skills fall into two categories. Firstly, there are the routine tests that therapists and teachers use to ascertain the appropriate starting place for therapy or to review a training program. Providing the obvious general precautions are applied, such as a picture-based test is not given to someone with a severe visual impairment, these are generally very useful.

Secondly, there are tests devised to ascertain whether an individual is communicating in particular circumstances, or with specific individuals, or whether a specific communication is valid. As there are no standard tests for this purpose, procedures have to be devised on an ad hoc basis. The basic rules for testing still apply: be sure of what (and whom) you are testing, and make sure the person with severe communication impairments has the equipment, training, and motor and sensory skills necessary to undertake the test.

Possible issues and examples for examination by such testing include the following:

1. *Environmental*—Is Joe using his communication book appropriately when he travels on public transport?
2. *Personnel*—Do Mary and Fred have the skills necessary to receive and relay Joe's communication accurately?
3. *Authenticity*—Did Joe really say Bill stole his watch?
4. *Veracity*—Was Joe right when he said Bill stole his watch?
5. *Ability*—Can Joe communicate in a particular mode or at a particular level?

To Joe, the fifth question is obviously most important. It is equally important to note that on any particular occasion the answers to questions 1,2,3, and 4 could all be "no" without affecting the answer to question 5. Joe can be using his aid wrong, and Mary and Fred could be poor facilitators, and they could have gotten Joe's message wrong, or Joe could be lying, and it could still be true that in the right circumstances with a good facilitator Joe could spell out exactly what he wanted. In particular, it's important not to confuse authenticity and veracity. People with severe communication impairments, just like the rest of us, give incorrect information for a wide variety of reasons—love of invention, malice, poor pragmatics—but, unlike the rest of us, people sometimes assume that if what people with severe communication impairments are saying isn't true then it can't have been them saying it.

Strategies for obtaining answers to each of the questions will vary. How much effort is devoted to answering such questions should depend on circumstances. If an 8-year-old's integration aide helps her with her spelling test this is not a major issue—in fact, it might be excellent educational practice. In grades 11 and 12, it becomes more important to know who is doing the work, the student or the aide, and it may be necessary to validate the student's work with the particular partner or partners who are going to assist in exams.

Specific circumstances may require special tests. Joe may have to prove that he has the ability to make and communicate decisions. Whatever procedures used should take into account specific problems Joe may have—if he has a word-finding problem, even a simple test like being asked the names of family members may not be appropriate. If Joe requires a communication partner with specific skills—a sign interpreter, say, or a facilitator—every effort should be made to use the person with whom Joe is believed to communicate most competently (ideally, of course, the partner should be Joe's own choice). Otherwise the outcome may be affected by the ineptitude of an unskilled or unfamiliar partner. Finally, Joe should be told the general nature of the test procedure, so he can practice any specific skills required, such as using headphones or passing messages.[1]

On another occasion—if Joe is making a will, for example—it may be necessary to verify Joe's communication through a particular communication partner. Ideally, in such a case more than one partner would be involved—two sign language interpreters could be used simultaneously, or two facilitators could be used sequentially, with Joe repeating his wishes.

If any of the questions 1–5 are answered negatively it is important to take remedial action, as would be taken with a person who fails a conventional assessment. Learning communication skills is like learning to drive—there is a continuum of skill and skills that can be improved. If we fail a driving test we take more lessons and practice, then we have another go. We are not stopped from driving altogether.

LEARNED HELPLESSNESS

The effect on an individual of having a long-term, unremedied communication impairment needs to be taken into account in any assessment. Such individuals are unlikely to be confident in everyday interactions. They are likely to have experienced much failure and frustration. They may have negative attitudes to assessment as the result of past experiences with inappropriate testing strategies and are unlikely to have the communication skills or assertiveness to make their concerns known to the examiner. Without a great deal of encouragement they may be unwilling even to try at the test and may just answer at random in order to get the procedure over with as quickly and painlessly as possible.

ASSESSMENT AT DEAL

Whatever we feel about testing, we do have to find out information about what people do and do not know, and can and cannot do, so we can make worthwhile suggestions about future programs. The assessment that follows is merely an attempt to generate the maximum relevant information in the minimum time. It is by no means the perfect solution to assessment problems. It is included here as an example of an alternative approach, that has proved effective with some people.

The standard assessment used at DEAL for children whose speech clearly needs augmentation is based around an educational toy with voice output called My Talking Computer. The toy has two booklets associated with it. When a page of a booklet is keyed up a pleasant (American) female voice asks a random set of five questions about whatever is represented on the page. The questions are answered by pressing the appropriate item on the page (and consequently the test is unsuitable for children who cannot use their hands, with whom other strategies are used). After five questions a score is given, and if all questions have been answered correctly music is played. By selecting appropriate pages it is possible to check picture recognition, knowledge of concepts such as shape, size, and color, and word and letter recognition. One sheet allows the user to compose their own sentence or story from written words and have it spoken by the toy. While the information about specific knowledge is interesting, really only picture and word recognition and the ability to compose a sentence are important in terms of future communication intervention.

The observational data generated by the student's interaction with the toy are at least as important as the information obtained about their knowledge of concepts. The initial responses of students confronted both by the toy and my expectation of task completion were variable. My Talking Computer was chosen as an assessment

tool because it does not look at all like a standard test, it is easily
portable (so can be administered on the floor if the student refuses
to sit at a table), and most children find the voice output very motivating. Most importantly, no speech is required to respond to the
questions, and no complex motor skills are needed—simple pointing is all that is required. Many autistic children respond to this
assessment more positively than they have been reported as
responding to any structured task previously. Some attempt to
reject it in the same way as they have been reported as rejecting
any structured task. Most students maintain concentration for
longer periods than has been reported previously.

The most useful information gained from the assessment is
generated by the student's attempt(s) to respond to the first question on the first page of pictures. That is, information on how the
student uses his/her hands and eyes. If the student points with a
whole hand, without isolating an index finger, that will be corrected, either by an oral prompt or by the tester shaping the student's hand with her hand. If the student uses two hands and hits
two answers at once one hand will be restrained. A student who
points without looking will be restrained from pointing until his
or her eyes are on task. Any other hand function problems will
also be remedied if observed at this stage, generally by the tester
using her hands to facilitate the student in the production of purposeful responses.

As the assessment proceeds other information will be generated
about hearing, auditory discrimination, receptive language, visual
acuity and scanning, perseveration, impulsivity, concentration,
auditory memory (one sheet asks the user to find "the small red tri-
angle"), and sequencing (in the sentence composition task). Every
effort is made to enable the student to achieve "success," especially
on the earlier sheets, as this may encourage the student to try
harder when they reach the later word recognition tasks. A student
who clearly does not know the correct answer to a question will be
assisted to find it by the tester. The toy will then give the student
positive feedback "You're right!" although the response will be
recorded by the tester as not being the student's.

In testing it is important to differentiate between facilitation,
which allows the student to make the choice, and assistance or
direction which leads the student to make a response chosen by the
tester. A student whose hand is molded by the tester in order to
achieve index finger isolation may make clear purposeful choices,
that will be recorded as the student's own. Another student may
not need any hands-on facilitation but may need oral cueing to

achieve success. These cued responses will not be recorded as the student's own choices, even though the student pointed without any physical assistance.

The assessment is not scored—its use is the information that it generates, which is recorded as comments on the record sheet. This assessment does not terminate if a student does not show some of the early skills. A student may have no knowledge of shape names and therefore be unable to succeed on the three sheets that include shapes. Indeed, if the ignorance was obvious on the first shape sheet, the next two sheets would be omitted. That does not mean that the same student may not have word recognition skills. In fact, sometimes students who have performed reluctantly, with ambiguous results, on earlier sheets. improve concentration and performance markedly on sheets containing written words. If the student shows no sign of word recognition skills by the end of the sheet containing twelve written words then the Talking Computer assessment would be terminated, and other tasks would be substituted.

All students who show word recognition skills will be given a chance to use a keyboard, regardless of whether they appear to recognize the names of upper case letters. Any students who are so uncooperative as to make it hard to be sure what they do know are also given access to a keyboard. On several notable occasions students who refused even to sit on a chair to work with My Talking Computer have become perfectly cooperative when given a chance to type, and have shown functional spelling skills. Access to the keyboard is given using whatever level of facilitation has been determined to be necessary during the earlier part of the assessment. Most commonly the Canon Communicator is used in the initial assessment because it is durable, easily portable and has a keyguard to stop the typist's finger from hitting more than one key at a time. Output consists of large upper case letters printed on thin strips of paper tape.

A student who shows functional spelling skills at this stage, that is, the ability to spell a recognizable sentence without a model, will probably be able to augment speech with typing. If they are unable to type without facilitation they are then candidates for facilitated communication training. Facilitated communication training may also be used with students who do not show any literacy skills but who require facilitation to point to pictures or symbols in order to augment their speech. Students who plan to augment their speech with typing will undertake formal and informal reading assessments. A selection of expressive and receptive language assessments is available and will be administered as appropriate by a speech pathologist or teacher if the information generated is judged necessary for future intervention. No one is tested simply for the sake of testing—there is no point in giving a girl with an oral vocabulary of five words a word-finding test that exposes her to unnecessary failure and generates no useful information. However, a test of receptive language, such as the Peabody Picture Vocabulary Test, may be relevant for this girl (if she can point reliably) as it could enable her to demonstrate that her comprehension of oral language is well in excess of her spoken language, and could give an indication of the appropriate level for communication augmentation.

CONCLUSION

All this may make it seem that accurate assessment of people with severe communication impairments is impossible. It is not impossible—it just requires time and patience (even the fastest typist types at a quarter the speed of a speaker) and a willingness to depart from standardized tests that are not standardized on this population. The goal of assessment is always to find out what individuals can do, not what they can't. It is especially important to keep that in mind when assessing people with severe communication impairments.

As Heisenberg said, "What we observe is not nature itself but nature exposed to our method of questioning." For anyone to be justly labeled as intellectually impaired we must know enough about brain function to be able to examine "intelligence" unaffected by input restrictions caused by impairment or nurture and to assess intellectual functioning uninfluenced by expressive impairments. If we are unable to do so, we should not label people who cannot answer our questions as intellectually impaired.

ENDNOTES

[1] Message passing always seems straightforward to people who can talk, who have passed on messages since preschool. An adult who has just started to use nonspeech communication may never have passed on a message before and may feel quite unsure about what he or she should do. Message passing will be impossible if the person with severe communication impairments has short-term memory impairments. It should always be checked that the person can repeat a message after a short time lag before using this as a testing strategy.

10

Who Said That?

＊＊＊

There are many systems of communication that don't involve speech. All of them have problems of interpretation.

The most widely used substitute for speech is deaf sign. People who use deaf sign are comparatively lucky. Signing is the oldest and best-known nonspeech system. Translation and checking procedures acceptable to users have been developed, and there is a large number of potential interpreters available. Despite these advantages, even fluent sign users have problems being understood by most speakers.

People who use other modes of nonspeech communication have even more problems in getting their words accepted. In part this is because these methods are relatively new (communication boards with pictures and symbols have been used for only 20 years, deaf sign for 200) and in part it is because of the wide variability between users and systems. Sign users may share little more than their deafness, but at least they share that. People who use other nonspeech communication strategies do not even share a common diagnosis—they may have cerebral palsy, for example, Down syndrome, autism, motor neuron disease, intellectual impairments, or acquired brain damage.

The communication strategies used by nonspeakers are as varied as their diagnoses. At the easy end of the scale, a relatively small number of individuals can communicate by writing or typing without any assistance other than provision of appropriate equipment. These people have relatively little difficulty in getting their messages across, although there may still be problems caused by the comparative slowness of written communication and its lack of intonation.

All nonspeech communication is very laborious compared with speech. A speaker may talk at a rate of 150 words per minute. The fastest nonspeaker is unlikely to achieve 30 words per minute and few would achieve more than 10. The physical effort and concentration involved in generating those words is many times greater than that involved in speech, and consequently nonspeech communication cannot be sustained for lengthy periods.

If the communication is typed it can be exact but will suffer from lack of intonation—the added meaning speakers give by tone of voice and facial expression, and that signers emulate with vivid hand movements. It may also suffer from being taken too seriously and "over-interpreted," because in our culture written communication is always given heavier weight than spoken, and what in speech would be a throw-away line or a slip of the tongue may, if typed, be subject to detailed analysis.

More problems occur when individuals use systems with limited vocabularies and/or require the assistance of communication partners to get out their messages. John uses a VOCA (voice output communication aid) independently; however, the aid only contains 32 utterances, and if John wants to communicate about anything not covered in those 32 utterances he has to use approximations or answer yes/no questions. John, like other users of limited vocabulary systems, requires a questioner with the skill to elucidate the meaning of his selection. A symbol board, for example, is likely to have one symbol for all the tenses of a verb. If a user points to RUN, does he mean "I ran," "I was running," or "I wanted to run" or "Run!"?

If nonspeaking people require some form of physical assistance or facilitation in order to use a communication aid the question often arises as to whether the words are theirs.

Facilitated communication *training* is a teaching strategy used to help people with severe communication impairments develop the hand skills needed to use communication aids independently. The ultimate validation of the technique is to bring people to the stage where they can use their aids without facilitation.

WHEN TO VERIFY COMMUNICATION

Most individuals with severe communication impairments will never need the consistency of individual communications to be validated formally (informal validation will take place, as it does for speaking individuals, in everyday interactions). The most obvious way to check the consistency of communication is to have the individual discuss the same topic on different occasions and/or with different partners. If they do so, and what they communicate is similar on each occasion, that means they are consistent, and the partners did not imagine or misinterpret the communication (although it still does not mean the communication is correct—the individual may just be consistently wrong).

There are, however, certain situations where it is important to investigate the skills of users of nonspeech communication or their communication partners:

1. There may be some dispute about a person's communication skills in relation to a serious matter.
   Joe, who has cerebral palsy, needs surgery, and it is doubtful whether his communication through his symbol board is adequate for him to give informed consent.

2. There may be some dispute about the influence of a particular facilitator or communication partner on a person's communication in relation to a serious matter.
   It's accepted that Mary, who has motor neuron disease, can communicate using a Canon Communicator with arm support. Mary is very fond of her brother John. John says that Mary wants to give him a large sum of money. There is concern that when Mary is typing with John as her facilitator he influences the communication.

3. In a particular situation there may be a need for a particular communication partner to establish that they have the skills needed to enable a person to communicate without help or hindrance.
   George is studying for his final school exams. He usually communicates with little or no facilitation by typing on an adapted keyboard; however, the mathematics he is studying cannot be done on a typewriter keyboard, and he will have to use a special communication board with facilitation. It is thus important to ascertain that his facilitator does not influence his answers, and that, on the other hand, his facilitator has enough mathematical knowledge to be able to transcribe his answers in the appropriate format.

These three needs for verification are all noncontroversial, and all clearly benefit the communication aid user. A dispute about whether the individual can communicate at all is adversarial, and different considerations apply.

The best way of establishing the level of receptive and expressive language available to the individual is a detailed speech-language assessment by a therapist with experience in both nonspeech communication and the individual's disability. The role of such an assessment is to establish levels of communication. It starts with a presumption that the individual is able to communicate, and endeavors to establish the extent of that communication.

Occasionally a speech-language assessment will show that an individual's skills have been overestimated—it is possible to interpret randomly hit symbols or letters as a meaningful utterance, or to "improve" someone's communication. More often, such an assessment will show that the nonspeaker's skills have been underestimated or underused. Though the last decade has seen enormous advances in the techniques and technology used to assist individuals with severe communication impairments, these have not yet come into widespread use. The large majority of nonspeakers are not receiving specialist intervention and are likely to have undeveloped communication potential.

No one should be blamed for overestimating or underestimating the nonspeaker's skills—but every effort should be made to find strategies that do enable the individual to communicate and participate in decision making to the best of his or her capacity.

Excluding the possibility of partner influence is difficult and time consuming. It is only necessary if the communication aid user is going to take an exam or give evidence and needs an accredited communication partner. Other statements can be checked more satisfactorily by using multiple partners than by accrediting one partner. The problem of verification in such cases is obviously reduced if the nonspeaking person can hear or read and can unambiguously signal yes and no, in that then they can be asked whether the utterance produced is indeed what they wanted to say.[1] Unfortunately, while most people using facilitated communication can read or hear, many do not have clear and unambiguous ways of indicating yes and no without using their communication aids.

In serious matters an independent facilitator or interpreter should be involved as early as possible (with the permission of the nonspeaking person):

1. in order to validate the original facilitation or translation (a check on accuracy and replicability)
2. to ensure the nonspeaking person has an opportunity to communicate via someone with no interest in the case (a check on undue influence)

3. to assess the practical and legal problems involved in the person giving evidence if court proceedings are involved.

In some instances it will be discovered that there is no communication partner available who is not involved in the matter at issue. What to do in this situation is a matter of judgment. If the matter is important, or court proceedings are likely, the only solution may be to train another communication partner (again, with the nonspeaker's consent).

No qualification such as an interpreter's certificate exists in nonspeech communication, and even if it did, the range of communication systems and individual variations is so great that it is difficult to imagine that one individual could hope to have the skills to assist all nonspeakers. Because a common system of nonspeech communication does not and cannot exist, most nonspeaking people who do not type or write have a relatively small number of people to whom they can communicate freely. People who are deaf have gained the right to use the interpreter of their choice in court, and this precedent should be applied to the situation of people without speech; everyone has his or her own communication style, and it is easier to get your message across to, or via, some people than others. If the impartiality of the chosen communication partner is an issue, other strategies for checking the communication aid user's output may need to be used.

The most common reason to try and ensure that communication partners are not affecting the student's output (for better or for worse[2]) is of course the needs of the classroom. If the partner needs specialist knowledge, such as the ability to set out math problems, then that should be checked by the math teacher or some other appropriate specialist. If the concern is to ensure that the student is able to do the work various strategies may be used.

May took her final economics exam with a communication partner who had left school at age 15 and never studied economics. Tina, who types *very* slowly and laboriously without facilitation, did one exam question without facilitation and the rest with facilitation; all her answers were of a similar standard and it was accepted that this did represent Tina's real level of achievement. Marc needs facilitation to type but can point to multiple choice answers without facilitation—his exam answers were checked by the administration of a multiple choice test. Bob typed his history essays with different facilitators; however, the standard and style of all the essays were consistent, and were different from the styles of his facilitators.

Strategies such as these may help convince other people that the work is the student's own, but in the end the issue is likely to come down to the integrity of the facilitators, as it does in any situation where a student is working closely with another person—an amanuensis, for example, or a deaf interpreter. It is important to ensure that the student is not further disadvantaged in the search for verification. May passed her exams and applied for university entrance, but one university said they would accept her only if she did an additional test, devised by a psychologist, to prove she could type. At the other end of the scale, when Sam, aged 6, was using a typewriter for the first time his integration aide was not allowed to facilitate him for fear she might help him! In both cases the compulsion to test outweighed the central purpose of education, which is to teach.

ADVERSARIAL TESTING

The fourth situation in which verification of communication is required comes about when someone is affronted by something the communication aid user has said, or, indeed, affronted by the very suggestion that they can communicate anything at all. Anne McDonald was admitted to an institution at the age of 3 and labeled as profoundly retarded. When she turned 18 and said she wanted to leave, the Health Commission opposed her departure on the grounds she could not communicate. Anne's application for Habeas Corpus was heard in the Supreme Court; the presumption of competence applied, and she was released without special testing. She is now in the process of completing a degree in humanities. "Carla" was labeled as severely intellectually impaired. In her 20s, she alleged that family members had mistreated her. She was given elaborate validation tests. The results of these tests were presented to the Guardianship Board, which decided that she was unable to communicate. After the case her family withdrew Carla from her day program, and she lost her means of communication.

The cases of Anne and Carla have several elements in common; neither woman can speak, both used communication aids to say things that their caregivers did not want to hear, and in both cases the caregivers responded by denying that the women had any ability to communicate. Each case was adversarial, in that there were individuals involved who hoped or believed that Anne/Carla could not communicate. Anne could do nothing independently, and was totally dependent on testing to demonstrate her capacity. Eventually, she passed a validation test and a reading test (the Health Commission tried to hide the test results, but they came out in court). Carla was also given tests, and failed them. She could have demonstrated her capacity by using a communication aid independently, but the Guardianship Board refused to see her do so. At the end of the day the common law served Anne well, and the special system devised for people with disabilities served Carla badly. If Anne had been ssubjected to the same tests as Carla, would she have been released? If Carla had not been tested, would any harm have been done[3]—any harm, at least, comparable to what has occurred to Carla as the result of her test failure?

In adversarial validation only one question is being asked: Can the person use his/her communication aid or strategy effectively? There will be a number of people involved who hope he or she cannot. Tests may be administered or suggested by people who hope the aid user will fail. Hostile observers may be present at testing sessions. In most cases[4] the aid user has everything to lose and nothing to gain from test participation. If they pass, nothing will change. If they fail, they may lose what little in the way of communication they have.

Testing performed incompetently can have tragic effects. A test that does not take into account the life experience of the people being tested, however objective it may look, will still be unfair. Seventy years ago the Australian Immigration Department enforced a discriminatory policy of excluding certain racial groups. It did this through a simple objective measure—the dictation test. Under the Immigration Act any potential migrant could be asked to undertake a dictation test. This was, on the face of it, a measure designed to guard against the admission of illiterates. However, the Act didn't specify the language of the test. People whose skin wasn't the right color were given tests in languages they didn't know, and when they failed the test they were excluded. Indian professors educated at Oxford failed tests in Gaelic. For every one of us, there are more tests we will fail than tests we can pass.

If this is true for people without disabilities, it is much more true for people with disabilities. Whether people with disabilities are able to demonstrate their skills will to a large extent depend on the type of tests they are given. Anne, a quadriplegic, was assessed as profoundly intellectually impaired on a test that required her to build a 3-block tower. Karen, a schoolgirl with cerebral palsy, failed the end-of-year tests because her teacher refused to let her use a typewriter on the grounds that it would give her an unfair advantage. An unfair disadvantage, apparently, was no problem.

Because you haven't seen something doesn't mean it doesn't exist. That oyster doesn't look like the kind that has pearls, most oysters don't have pearls, I've never seen an oyster with a pearl in it; all of these statements may be true, but they still do not prove that there *isn't* a pearl in *this* oyster or that this oyster could not produce a pearl in the future. It is vital to remember this when testing someone's ability to communicate. The aid user may not have proved that he or she can communicate. You certainly have not proved that they cannot ever communicate.

The issues of consent and cooperation are central in adversarial testing. As a general rule people should not be tested without their consent. Every effort should be made to obtain informed consent before testing. Obviously there will be problems if consent can only be given or withheld by using the contested communication strategy. However, if an individual is held not to be competent to *refuse* consent, he or she is correspondingly incompetent to *give* consent. Whatever the consent situation, it must be recognized that testing undertaken without cooperation is valueless.

Because of these considerations, and because validation testing is complex, time consuming, and stressful, it is advisable to look for evidence of communication in everyday interactions before resorting to formal tests. The individual's everyday communication may be examined for evidence that indicates that the words are theirs. Does the person always talk about certain topics, or use specific idioms, or misspell certain words regardless of who is facilitating? Prue has a very individualistic style, starting a high proportion of sentences with adverbs and using certain favorite idioms and words such as. "weird," frequently, regardless of who her communication partner is. Does the person tell his facilitators things they could not know otherwise, things that have happened when they weren't around? When Joe told me that they'd had a bad trip down because they'd nearly hit a car, and his driver said that was true, this validated Joe's communication.

Too often this form of validation is overlooked. This is unfortunate because a few instances of successful communication are much more significant than many "failures." If Joe hadn't told me about the near-accident there would have been many possible explanations—he'd forgotten, he didn't want to embarrass the driver, he didn't think it important, he couldn't find the right words, etc. But when Joe *did* tell me about it there was only *one* possible explanation; he was communicating, and I was receiving the communication.

If such instances of incidental validation do not occur spontaneously it may be possible to structure a situation to make them more likely. Gina was being asked to name pictures not seen by her facilitator and was not doing very well. An hour and a half after testing had started, she spontaneously typed something about wanting ANOTHER PRESENT. She went on to tell her facilitator that the psychologists undertaking the testing had given her a candy before the testing started. This was confirmed, and provided much better evidence of her ability to convey information unknown to her facilitator than her performance on the confrontational naming task.

If the aid used is a typewriter or alphabet board, the basic skills involved are reading and spelling. Reading skills may be demonstrated by administering standard assessments that do not involve use of a communication aid or facilitation—the administration, for example, of multiple choice reading tests such as the Reading Comprehension Battery for Aphasia (LaPointe, 1984).

If a demonstration of spelling skills is necessary, and the person is not able to select letters without facilitation, then there are informal procedures available that may be appropriate in some cases—answering a question or passing a message not known to the facilitator, for example, or describing items that are out of sight of the facilitator. These strategies can also be used with symbol or sign based communication. If the issue is relatively straightforward—Ben's father does not believe he can really be typing, say, because his hand is being held—then successful use of such a strategy may well defuse the issue before it becomes a major concern. Before testing, especially in the early stages of a communication training program, it is important to explain that failing such a test does not mean that people cannot or will not be able to use that communication strategy. What it shows is that they or their facilitators do not currently have the skills necessary to pass that test.

Choosing the appropriate verification strategy will depend on factors such as visual and auditory memory, maturity, and language skills. The skills needed can be developed in regular teaching sessions and the procedures administered quickly, with minimal stress and no requirements for specialized settings or equipment. Facilitator competence will be a significant variable, as will the length of time the individual has been in the training program. Failures should be investigated and the tests repeated after further training, possibly in a different form or with a different facilitator.

Informal questioning can also be used to provide a useful indication of a facilitator's skills—I play "Telephone" with communication aid users who are known to have good skills, whispering messages for them to relay to their facilitators. Success boosts the confidence of the facilitator and failure indicates a need for more training before that facilitator is used for any important communication tasks. It is important that tests of student facilitators not be combined with tests of student aid users, because if the outcome is a "fail" it will not be clear who has failed, the user or the facilitator. Any testing for facilitator influence should only be undertaken after a user has demonstrated his or her basic capacity to use the communication system. Any facilitator used in formal validation testing should have previously demonstrated the ability to facilitate by successfully facilitating an aid user during informal testing.

WHEN TO VALIDATE

No communication partner or person with severe communication impairments should be asked to undergo formal validation testing until they have completed basic communication training (as assessed by the agency overseeing the communication program); otherwise all that negative results will show is that the person has not learned what they haven't been taught. Similarly, validation testing is completely inappropriate until the communication aid user is communicating freely and fluently with at least one partner. Facilitated communication training is, as its name implies, a *training* method. Training in nonspeech communication strategies takes *time*—therapists suggest that it can take 6 years for *basic* competence to be achieved in the use of communication aids without facilitation (Haney, 1988).

HOW TO VALIDATE

Validation Protocols

The assessment of communication, in any mode, is not normally the job of psychologists—certainly not of psychologists working in isolation. Any protocols for validation assessment of nonspeech communication should be developed by a multidisciplinary team with expertise in the various communication strategies to be assessed. Once developed the protocols should be circulated to relevant professional and consumer bodies for comment, and then amended if necessary. In Australia relevant bodies include AGOSCI (the Australian Group on Severe Communication Impairment), AASH (the Australian Association for Speech and Hearing), and CAUS (the Communication Aid User's Society). More than one validation strategy should be accredited, to cater for the different abilities and disabilities of people with severe communication impairments (some people cannot wear headphones, for example, and some people have short-term memory problems).

Preliminary Screening

Several assessments should be made before formal validation testing is undertaken:

- An assessment of hand function by an occupational therapist.
- A literacy assessment using a multiple-choice test.[5] The results of such a test would certainly have bearing on the future use of spelled communication, regardless of any negative results on validation testing.
- A speech/language assessment. If speech/language assessments are not made prior to testing it's impossible to know whether it would *ever* be possible for a given person to do the tests you are devising.

Preliminary Training

Trials at DEAL have shown that, with practice, most clients improve their performance on validation tasks. Performance improves, despite different questions each time, presumably because the clients become more at ease in the test situation and develop whatever skills are necessary to succeed. Practice of this nature is especially important if the chosen validation strategy involves significant interference with the procedures of everyday communication. For example, before anyone is given any test involving headphones, they need to practice receiving instructions through headphones. *If a person does not respond to everyday instructions given via headphones they should not be given test questions via headphones.* (Also, if they do not respond to everyday instructions given by a particular examiner they should not be given test questions by that examiner.) If the receiver only is to wear headphones, the receiver should practice wearing headphones in regular communication sessions with the person and observe what effect, if any, this has on communication.

Environment

The aid user should also be familiar with the environment in which the test will be conducted. Testing will ideally take place in the aid user's regular setting—school, day center, or residence.

The effects of environment were demonstrated in an Australian court case (Police v. Williams, 1990) when a witness who typed with facilitation was brought into court to show how she communicated. The prosecutor had previously seen the aid user type successfully while her facilitator looked away, but he had overlooked the influence of the courtroom and the presence of the accused on his witness. Her facilitator was asked to look away from the keyboard while the witness was typing. The witness also looked away from the keyboard (at the accused) and, not surprisingly, the result was rubbish.

People with severe communication impairments often have associated or secondary impairments that make them especially vulnerable in testing situations. The most obvious problem is lack of self-confidence together with lack of social experience—many people who can speak can be rendered mute by aggressive questioning. Anyone with spasticity could be rendered so tense as to preclude communication altogether. People with less well known problems may also have their ability to communicate accidentally or deliberately sabotaged. Some people with neurological damage have hyperactive startle reflexes—they go rigid (and some may actually convulse) when there is a sudden noise, such as the click of the switch on a tape recorder. Others are visually disinhibited; that is, they cannot stop themselves from looking toward anything that moves within their field of vision. Their communication would be affected if the observers kept shuffling their papers while they were trying to type or point.

Formal Validation Testing

The special needs of each person must be taken into consideration when devising validation testing. The person who does not have word-finding or recall problems may be able to respond to message passing as a method of validation, but not everyone can handle this particular test. Anne could, Carla could not. Some people require a cue to be constantly present; in these cases a tray of objects may be presented and one singled out for the person to point to or spell with the communication partner when he/she comes into the room. Others, who have difficulty with specificity, may be able to recount the general theme of a story that is read and visually tracked with them while their partners are out of the room. Or, they may be able to type a variety of words associated with a given theme such as "holiday" or answer questions about the attributes of pictures that their partners cannot see. Because word-finding problems are common, every effort should be made to avoid questions answered with names or nouns—"What can you do with it?" is a better question than "What is it?"

One frequent assumption, based on ignorance, is that if an aid user cannot pass messages they cannot communicate. That is a total absurdity. There are many people who can speak and/or type totally independently who cannot pass messages, or who can only pass messages after many rehearsals.

"Carla," who has major word-finding problems, was tested by three psychologists for 11 hours. The most significant test involved Carla answering 40 questions. The answer to every question was a noun. What are the hardest words for people with word-finding problems to retrieve? Nouns. When is it hardest for people with word-finding problems to retrieve nouns? When they are placed on the spot, and have to give a specific answer quickly. Carla failed the test. It might as well have been in Gaelic.[6]

It is vital when seeking validation of communication that several requirements be met:

1. The partner is trained and experienced with the facilitated communication method.
2. The aid user has previously communicated fluently with that partner.
3. The aid user is satisfied that there is a genuine reason for the validation being sought and gives consent to the procedure.
4. The aid user has experience with the validation task required and has demonstrated the skills required by the testing procedure.

Whatever the strategy used, arrangements must be made for frequent repetition of questions. This is vital because the process of spelling an answer is lengthy, and the short-term memory status of most people with severe communication impairments is unknown.

It must be emphasized that no one test can be given a special privileged status. If evidence is presented that purports to show that a person can communicate, there must be valid reasons given for disregarding it. It is not enough to say that any tests other than tests approved and administered by one team are invalid—evidence must be produced as to why they are invalid. Some tests, such as answering a question, naming a picture, or typing a given word completely unknown to the facilitator, have such a low probability of chance success that a single correct performance is enough to validate the person's ability to use his/her communication aid. Bruce was asked to tell his facilitator, who was out of hearing, the name of his house. The facilitator had no knowledge of the question, so when Bruce typed "I always have difficulty remembering the name of my house." that validated his ability to type with facilitation, as well as confirming that he had a word-finding problem.

The importance of one success needs to be emphasized, and may need careful explanation to people unfamiliar with testing null hypotheses. In adversarial situations there is a tendency to set arbitrary levels of performance that have nothing to do with the central question which is "Can this person prove he or she can use this communication aid by communicating one thing unknown to his or her communication partner?" Bruce was tested repeatedly—sometimes he answered questions correctly and sometimes he didn't. The people testing him seemed to be operating on the basis that a score of 50% was necessary for a pass. On his last test Bruce scored very badly. This score was seen as outweighing his earlier successes and he was judged to have failed validation.

VALIDATION—WHAT DO YOU DO WHEN SOMEONE FAILS A TEST?

One aspect of facilitated communication that causes concern is that of facilitator influence or cueing. To say that *all* of an individual's communication is tainted by facilitator influence it is necessary to test every facilitator that the individual has communicated with—it is not scientific to say that because it was shown that facilitator A cued the client's communication, therefore facilitators B, C, and D also cued communication. Even facilitator A may not be providing cues all the time.

It is important not to overreact. It must be recognized that we all influence each other, consciously and subconsciously. There is nothing horrifying or surprising in the discovery that two persons working together to try and establish communication under difficult circumstances will take cues from one another. This is only a cause for anxiety when it appears that *all* the communication of that person is created by cueing, or when particular (and important) utterances are suspected of having been cued. In any case, the discovery of cueing should be the signal for further training of both the person and their partner.

Carla was given an inappropriate test and failed. Unfortunately for Carla, it wasn't the dictation test and her failure didn't have the relatively minor penalty of not being able to live in Australia. Rather, she was isolated from her friends and from access to any nonspeech communication. We might as well have cut out her tongue. She will certainly never be able to complain.

Bruce's test results were misinterpreted and he was banned from typing. Again, he is unable to complain.

This raises the most important issue in testing. What do you do when someone fails? Again, it is important not to overreact. Failure on one test, or even several tests, does not prove that someone *cannot* use the communication strategy being tested. It is necessary to examine the variables, and see what could have gone wrong.

Did the person want to do the test—did they try? Was the test appropriate, or did it require language and memory skills that may be impaired? Was the facilitator up to the task? Was the person thrown by the whole procedure? How invasive was it? Had they ever done anything like this before? Allow more practice and change some of the variables. Meanwhile, look for everyday validation.

Most people who use facilitated communication will never have to go through any particular validation procedures. Some clients who now type independently were never called upon to validate their communication while they were receiving facilitation. Other clients who now type independently failed validation testing when they were facilitated. Doron did the same test as Carla and failed it. He refused to cooperate, in fact, and sat there typing "xxxxxxxxx" for half an hour. He went on to make his Bar Mitzvah, is now at the top of his high school class, and types, when he wants to, without anyone touching him or being in the room with him. What is important—his test result, or what he's done since? If his communication program had been terminated as a result of his test failure, he could not have made his Bar Mitzvah or undertaken the regular high school syllabus.

A psychologist asked me why Gina was in the facilitated communication training program. "She's talking pretty clearly and she points beautifully" he said. Yes, she does (though her speech is still not adequate for her to tell her facilitator that she'd been given a present, much less what it was). But she didn't when she started in the program 4 years ago! If she had been tested at the start of the program and failed what would it have proved—that she didn't have the skills that we were about to start teaching her? The answer to the question of what to do if someone fails should be to give them more training. This is an educational program. People won't have the skills at the start that we hope they will have at the end. The goal of facilitated communication training is independent use of a communication aid. The facilitation is used to remedy hand function impairments. These will not be remedied by withdrawing people from the program. The issue should not be the facilitation (though obviously that needs regular review, to ascertain whether users are improving) but the choice of communication aid/strategy.

It is absurd and unjust to deny someone access to communication training on the basis of failure on a given test. It is the equivalent of banning 18-year-olds from driving for life if they failed their first driving test. The communication program may have validity completely separate from the validation of a person's communication. Gina learned to point and her speech increased. Doron benefited by the increase in his attention span from a minute to an hour and the improvement in his eye/hand coordination. Maria started to initiate interactions for the first time.

We are just learning about the *real* language, memory, neuro-motor, and concentration impairments of people with severe communication impairments. These certainly affect their ability to undertake various kinds of tests. What we need to work toward is a situation where people take a rational attitude to people starting to communicate with facilitation and are prepared to work through the various problems that occur.

The content of specific communications may have to be treated with caution, pending proof that they did come from the aid user, but lack of proof is no reason to prevent the person continuing to use nonspeech communication. A variety of communication strategies may be used in the hope that the user will find one easier to confirm or to use independently than others. However, initial failure to validate communication using a particular strategy is no reason to drop that strategy from the list of options, especially if that strategy offers more communication potential in the long term. For instance, spelling is the only way in which people with severe communication impairments can say exactly what they want to say. Consequently, it is reasonable to expend considerable effort in developing spelling and typing skills in people with severe communication impairments—as much effort, at least, as is devoted to developing literacy skills in nondisabled children.

Because communication is so important—the most important need for humans after food, shelter, and love—the benefit of the doubt must always apply. Many speech impaired people spend a life time being tested and asked to comply with the wishes/instructions of speaking people. Validation testing can be intimidating, stressful, and counterproductive—use it cautiously and sympathetically!

ENDNOTES

[1] This would in fact provide more verification than is usually available with foreign language or deaf sign interpretation, where in the nature of things there is no way to confirm with the speaker or signer that the translation is correct.

[2] It is most common for people to worry about the facilitator giving assistance, but the fact that facilitators can also *hinder* communication is often overlooked.

[3] Carla's allegations would have been left in the hands of the police, who would have been unlikely to proceed given the lack of confirmatory evidence.

[4] Anne McDonald was obviously an exception; she had more to gain than to lose. Interestingly, during a later Supreme Court case she objected strenuously to being tested, despite having everything to gain from completing tests that were far less arduous than Carla's.

[5] Print size and multiple choice presentation may need to be varied to cater for visual impairments and to allow for specific selection problems as shown in the OT assessment.

[6] To compound Carla's problems, 20 of the questions were asked via earphone, with no check that Carla could hear, and her facilitator was untrained and had no test experience.

11

Who Did What and to Whom— Limitations of Communication Without Speech

We all know the story of the boy who cried wolf—the shepherd boy who, bored with looking at nothing but a flock of the same old sheep, created a bit of drama and got some attention by pretending that there was a wolf attacking the flock. He tried it a couple of times and had everybody running in all directions very satisfactorily until the villagers eventually got wise and decided to ignore him. Unfortunately, the next time he cried "WOLF!" there really was a wolf, and the boy (and the villagers' sheep) were killed.

When children or people with disabilities say things we don't want to hear our problem as caregivers, teachers, and therapists is to sort out the real wolves from the pretend wolves. If real wolves are ignored, damage is done. If imaginary wolves are treated as real wolves, damage is done.

If we want to be able to distinguish between real and imaginary dangers we must understand the causes, the nature, and the consequences of severe communication impairments.

DISABILITY

The speech impaired person who uses augmentative (nonspeech) communication has an underlying disability such as autism, cerebral palsy, or Down syndrome. The use of augmentative communication may help the person to communicate more effectively but it does not cure the underlying disability.

The nature of the damage that caused their speech impairments means that some people with severe communication impairments have greater difficulty with some language tasks in all modalities than do speaking people. The ability to recall specific words—especially proper names—is impaired in many individuals. This difficulty may be due to word finding problems or to short-term memory loss. Some individuals with severe communication impairments appear to have problems attending to the detail of what they see in text or what they hear in conversation; thus they may get the general idea, but not the fine details of what they see or hear (not the first time round, at least).

COMMUNICATION SKILLS

Communication competence is not achieved simply through uttering sounds and words. It took us years to acquire this competence through daily activities that we took for granted but that helped to develop and strengthen our communication abilities. Our memory skills, for instance, were developed as children through activities such as getting things for other people ("John, can you get me two blue towels from the cupboard?"), relaying messages ("Tell daddy that dinner is ready"), and preparing for special events ("You'll need to pack your swim suit, zinc cream, and sunglasses for the picnic."). Nonspeaking children often do not have the means or the opportunity to practice these skills. Similarly, they do not experience the fun of participating with others in games and activities that test and challenge communication such as spelling bees, Chinese whispers (telephone), word-games, reciting rhymes, and singing songs, etc.

At the same time as we developed our skills in using words, we also developed our pragmatic skills—all the other skills, that is, associated with communication competence. We learned to look at the person we were talking to, or who was talking to us. We learned when to raise and lower our voices. We learned to be tactful. We learned to expand or change topics. We learned to reflect the content of our conversations in our facial expressions. We learned how to interrupt and when not to interrupt. We learned the consequences of exaggerating or telling lies. The list of pragmatic communication skills goes on and on.

Some of the skills on that list are difficult for people with specific disabilities—people who have difficulty controlling their facial muscles, for example, will not necessarily match their expressions with what they are saying. Other skills are impossible for communication aid users, regardless of their disability. A communication board cannot shout or whisper. You cannot look at the person you are talking to if you have to keep your eyes on a keyboard. Other skills are not impossible, but are acquired by experience. A novice communication aid user will not have that experience, and may take years to acquire it. The realities of nonspeech communication are that few communication aid users have the chance to communicate more than a few hundred words a day; the equivalent, that is, of 2 or 3 *minutes* of normal speech. Consequently, the usual time taken to acquire communication competence will be extended.

We tend to view everyone through the glass of our own experience, and we assume that an 18-year-old who has never spoken is the same as an 18-year-old who has lost his voice. This is quite incorrect. Whatever the primary disability, it is highly likely that the teenager with severe communication impairments will have learned and experienced language very differently from a nondisabled speaking person. Besides affecting the development of pragmatic skills, this also affects the development of specific communication skills. For example, a teenager or adult with severe communication impairments may never have been able to pass messages, or to give explanations, and these communication skills may have to be learned by the novice communication aid user at a relatively advanced age. The teenager may never have had a means of asking or answering questions, and so is likely to have gone through childhood without the numerous rehearsals of basic information to which questioning gives access.

It is obvious that asking questions is an enormously powerful means of acquiring information. Young children without speech impairments produce an almost continuous stream of questions, which not only gives them access to information and vocabulary, but an opportunity to practice initiation, clarification, interaction, and listening skills. The ability to answer questions is equally as important. Firstly, it is empowering, enabling the child to make choices in response to questions such as "What would you like to drink?" Secondly, answering questions provides an opportunity to rehearse and review information, and to use attention, listening, and recall skills. How many times does a speaking child answer questions like "How old are you?" "When's your birthday?" and "Where do you live?" before they turn 6? Nonspeaking adolescents who never have been asked any such questions may have difficulty retrieving information never previously required (or possibly not acquired because of the difficulty of asking for it). The whole concept of providing accurate information to virtually anyone who asks for it, which was drummed into us as children "Speak when you're spoken to!" "Answer Mrs. Smith, now," may be completely foreign to them.

Communication is a sharing process of questioning, making statements, offering suggestions, and giving feedback. People who do not have speech or have limited speech are less able to initiate conversations, ask questions, reveal their personalities, and control social situations. Speech impaired people are often forced to take a submissive role in communication exchanges. Self-esteem and confidence can be affected markedly!

ALLEGATIONS—HANDLE WITH CARE

People with undeveloped or impaired communication skills, whether they are children or adults, often have difficulty getting their messages across. This is frustrating for them, and may irritate those around them, but generally it is no more than an annoyance; however, when the issue is important, the minor annoyance can become a major problem. One issue that seems to cause a disproportionate share of problems for communication aid users and their partners is mistreatment. The problem starts when an aid user apparently alleges that someone has done him wrong.

Such allegations may result from

1. real abuse
2. imagined abuse
3. fabricated abuse:
   a. fabricated by communication aid user
   b. fabricated by partner:
      i. accidentally
      ii. deliberately
4. misunderstanding.

In fact, many "allegations" probably result from misunderstanding.

When we think of the number of times each day we have to ask for more information or explain or confirm utterances, and how often we still misunderstand or are misunderstood, it should be no surprise to learn that any form of nonspeech communication is vulnerable to misunderstanding. Misunderstanding is especially likely when novice aid users are communicating to novice partners. We can say "That's not what I meant" and "I beg your pardon." but the nonspeaking individual often can't. They may not have the skills, vocabulary, or confidence to do so. The balance of power in non-speech interactions is very much with the speaking partner and it is generally not easy for the nonspeaker to correct a misunderstanding. Individuals who are especially powerless are those who depend on the direct participation of the speaker to get a message out. Mike used an eye-pointing board. He wanted to tell the nurse he would like to go swimming tomorrow. He got as far as I WANT TO GO SWIMMING when the nurse, thinking she had the message, walked away taking the eye-pointing board with her.

The types of misunderstanding possible are many and various. If an individual is using a communication system with a limited vocabulary, the misunderstanding may occur because the user has to make one symbol stand for many concepts, and may only be able to utter black and white opinions, such as "I hate swimming" as opposed to qualified opinions "I don't like swimming if the water is cold." The limited vocabulary may not allow the composition of grammatically accurate sentences. Teresa's mother was worried after a party when 17-year-old Teresa pointed to "boy bad night dance." She would not have worried in the same way if Teresa had had the vocabulary to say exactly what she meant which was "The boys were mean last night and wouldn't dance with us."

Spelling is not restricted in the same way; spellers can "say" anything they can spell recognizably. Nonetheless, there are still problems of interpretation. Many of these occur because written language comes without intonation and body language. A transcript of an everyday spoken conversation is often hard to understand, because it only contains part of the information transferred. It doesn't include intonation, volume, or body language, or the nod of comprehension that led to a sentence being abbreviated. Like the transcript, all nonspeech communication (except manual signing) is bereft of emphasis.

When we read written language we impose our emphasis. Think of the simple sentence "I had some cake." It has four words and you can read it four ways:

> *I* had some cake (but Mary didn't).
> I *had* some cake (so don't bother offering me any more).
> I had *some* cake (but I wouldn't mind some more).
> I had some *cake* (but I wouldn't mind a biscuit).

If a communication aid user spells it to you, context and facial expression *may* make the meaning clear. If not, you either impose your interpretation or ask questions to elucidate the message. Misinterpretation in relation to a slice of cake is a minor annoyance; however, virtually every communication using graphic symbols or spelling is vulnerable to similar misinterpretation. It is very important for communication partners to read each message back and check that the interpretation they have placed on the message is the one the communication aid user intended.

Written communication is vulnerable in other ways. Speech disappears. Say something and it's gone. Unless someone records it, it can't come back to haunt you. Unfortunately that's not true of written communication. Tapes can be passed around, mulled over, taken completely out of context, when, because written language does not have facial expression, it is especially easy to misinterpret. (At least if speech was recorded it would still have intonation, and you could gather the surrounding context.) Liz takes the last cake. I say "I hate Liz"—no problem, especially if I smile. However, I type I HATE LIZ and the tape can be passed round, read hours or days after the original incident, and interpreted to mean that I don't want to live with Liz any more. Many people take typing at face value, without questioning the typist about what they mean. The fewer words the person has typed the more dangerous this is. If I type I HATE LIZ BECAUSE SHE TOOK THE LAST CREAMPUFF WHICH I HAD BEEN SAVING TO HAVE WITH MY COFFEE it doesn't matter if the tape is passed around, because the nature and triviality of the interaction are apparent.

The tendency to take everything that is typed too seriously also causes problems. At my suggestion Sal was given an 18-inch plastic rod by her day center, with the idea that she could hold it in her palm while she typed. I thought that this would help her isolate her index finger and perhaps avoid the need for a facilitator to hold her hand. At her residential unit the supervisor found the rod in Sal's bag and asked her what it was for. Sal made the mistake of making a joke. She typed that she had got the rod to bash the supervisor and another resident. The supervisor took Sal's typing to her superior and Sal was thrown out of the house on the grounds that she had threatened staff and residents!

This leads to another obvious limitation. Typing is slow. People often confuse the length of the message with the length of time it took to produce. A beginning typist may type fewer than 150 words in an hour. Because it took an hour, inexperienced professionals, who tend to be busy people (teachers, doctors, social workers, police, lawyers, etc.), tend to equate the output with what *we* would say in an hour. In fact, 150 words is the equivalent of only a minute's speech, and you wouldn't find police taking a case to court on the basis of a minute's speech. When considering whether further questioning is warranted before taking any action on an allegation, it is important to consider the quantity of material on which the supposed allegation rests rather than the time it took to obtain it.

People may be naive about the amount of time even a routine conversation can take. Pam, who is autistic, was admitted to a psychiatric unit when her behavior went out of control. The doctor wanted her consent to a medication change. He was appalled to discover that it took him 2 hours to get it, not because Pam was uncooperative, but because she had some questions she wanted to ask about the new medication. As he said later, the whole procedure would not have taken more than a few minutes if Pam had been able to speak. Questioning a communication aid user about a serious allegation may take considerably longer. Everyone involved needs to be aware of this and the necessary time needs to be provided if injustices are to be avoided.

Unfortunately speaking people are often diffident about questioning individuals with severe communication impairments, possibly because they feel sorry for the individuals and feel that to question them is unfair, that it suggests disbelief. Some of this diffidence probably relates to the pragmatic issues mentioned above. People find it difficult to conduct a conversation with someone who doesn't make eye contact or display the appropriate body language or throw the conversational ball back in the ordinary way.

Before acting on any allegation, it is important to have the answers to a lot of questions, like "Is that what you meant to say?" "What do you mean by that?" "Is this true?" as well as the obvious questions as to who, what, when, and where. Some individuals relate dreams or fantasies, either because they think them to be true, or think them interesting. The fantasy aspect may only come out during detailed questioning when for example the question "Who was there?" might be followed by the response "Hannibal Lecter!" Until such details are obtained, it is absurd to proceed on an allegation. Unfortunately, the problems of severe communication impairment combined with the impatience or inexperience of interviewers means that any such information may be obtained by leading questions or, even worse, questions just requiring a "yes" or "no" response. This is very dangerous, as many people with life-long disabilities have learned compliance, and may tend to agree with whatever is put to them.

In interpreting output, people often overlook the skewed experiences of many people with severe communication impairments. Unable ever to ask questions or take part in peer-group conversations they may have a pretty funny idea of what the world is all about. Lyn, a young adult, typed that a policeman had raped her mother. Fortunately her partner did not react immediately, but questioned her further. It turned out that Lyn thought "raped" meant the same as "flirted with!" Many "allegations" may be the result of imperfect understanding of the meaning of the words used.

Some misunderstandings occur because partners arbitrarily decide when a communication is complete. I was rung recently by a teacher who said he thought he had a case of sexual abuse on his hands. A student had just typed to him that "Dad is fucking me." I suggested he go back and ask her if that was all she wanted to say. He rang back to say she had added "around" and gone on to complain about her father telling her off for inappropriate screaming!

There is another problem related to allegations that has nothing to do with nonspeech communication, but a lot to do with the society we live in. Currently there appears to be a heightened awareness of the possibility of sexual assault, especially sexual assault by caregivers. Many individuals working with people with disabilities appear to be very sensitive to any language of a sexual nature, possibly because they don't expect this language to be used by people who live "protected" lives. Mary wanted to try out some of the words she'd heard in the high school playground at recess, so she typed PRICK FUCK CUNT. Her integration teacher called the school counselor, who assumed the worst after asking "clarifying" questions such as "Whose was the cunt?" and "Whose was the prick?" produced the answers MARY and DAD. Later the speech pathologist ascertained that Mary understood the question structure "Whose was the . . . ?" to mean "Who has a . . . ?"

Unfortunately, people's responses to nonspeech communication in any form are often irrational. Many people seem to believe that because something was typed it is true, and that if it is shown to be untrue then that means the person can't type. The third option, that the person can type, but tells lies or makes mistakes just like other people, is frequently overlooked. Bound up with this is our society's attitude to written language, which is generally taken as more serious, more considered than speech. Australian and American police have acted on typed material that they would have dismissed out of hand if it had been spoken.

READING HANDS, NOT MINDS

Another example of willingness to give more credence to something if it's typed is the belief in telepathy that has recently appeared in a few centers where facilitated communication is used. Typically one or more facilitators believe that one or more aid users are reading their thoughts. Sometimes the facilitators have asked the aid users if they are telepathic and have been told "yes."

A similar incident involving a DEAL client, "Jill," arose some years ago. Jill was attending a regular secondary school when some of the facilitators who worked with her in class said she was "getting into their thoughts." Jill's mother also thought she was telepathic and gave examples of situations in which Jill had typed out information that was only known to her. At this stage Jill was receiving only minimal facilitation from her mother, generally typing just with her mother's hand on her knee. When I asked Jill and her mother to demonstrate Jill's "telepathy" it became clear that Jill was picking up physical cues from her mother. Unconsciously Jill's mother was moving her hand toward the next letter she expected Jill to hit in an effort to speed up her typing, in the same way as a passenger may press a nonexistent accelerator or brake to speed up or slow down an incompetent driver. As she thought Jill was telepathic she expected Jill to type what she was thinking, so the process became self-reinforcing.

Jill admitted that she had been trying to get cues from her school facilitators, who held her wrist, initially so she could get the answers to school work, and then, once she discovered that it was possible, for fun. Jill knew a fair bit about her facilitators. She would introduce a likely topic into her typing—if they jumped to attention she would continue exploring it, if not she would erase the typing and it would just seem like a loss of concentration.

Jill's mother was quite distraught by this stage. She was worried that all the typing Jill had ever done had been cued, and that Jill had never been communicating. I knew this wasn't so, both because Jill had certainly never typed my thoughts and because of the development in her spelling and grammar over the years. To show her mother that she really could type Jill did some message-passing tests before going on to type completely independently, with no physical contact at all from her communication partners. The reports of Jill being telepathic stopped at this point.

Jill's story is instructive for several reasons. It shows how stories of telepathy can arise as the result of transmission of information from facilitator to aid user by subtle physical signals. Second, it was clear that Jill was far from a passive participant in the process—she actively sought cues and used her considerable literacy skills to capitalize on the cues she did pick up by using sophisticated word and sentence completion strategies. Third, "hand-reading" was a very rewarding activity for Jill—not only did she get excellent marks in school but her "paranormal" powers made her the center of attention. She happily went along with the story that she was telepathic until the school moved to disallow her exam results on the grounds that she had picked up the answers from her facilitators, and most facilitators refused to work with her because she was invading their privacy. Finally, the "hand-reading" was possible only because Jill was getting more support than she needed from her facilitators.

To date I have not heard of any examples of "telepathy" in facilitated communication training that cannot be explained by the processes that operated with Jill. In any instance where paranormal abilities are suggested for or by a communication aid user the first step should be to examine the facilitation process closely, both to see if a mechanism for transmission of information can be discerned and to see if the level of facilitation can be reduced. All facilitators involved should review their practices, referring back to the basic principles of facilitation, especially monitoring eye contact, pulling back, and reducing support. It is also important that new facilitators are not told to expect "telepathic" communication, because this expectation may lead them, as it did Jill's mother, to create it unconsciously.

DON'T THROW OUT THE BABY WITH THE BATHWATER

Nonspeech communication, in any mode, is limited and error prone when compared with speech. Very restricted communication is just as likely to produce problems as more fluent communication, but the problems will be different. Imperfect communication certainly produces problems for the person with communication impairments, but, unlike silence, it also produces problems for the rest of us. There is a real risk that our failure to handle the problems of imperfect communication may result in us imposing sanctions on people with severe communication impairments and disposing of our problems by shutting them up.

Facilitated communication training is a strategy for teaching people how to use communication aids. It does not cure anything. It is not a particularly good method of communication. However, it has allowed many individuals to communicate verbally for the first time in their lives. Communication involving facilitation is imperfect, but, for some people, right now it's the best option. Until we can find a better alternative, it is up to us to make facilitated communication work as well as possible.

Some basic principles for facilitators to follow are set out in Appendix C.

12

Case Studies

‹‹ ⊯⊹⊯ ››

CASE STUDY 1—IAN

Ian was almost 12 when his mother brought him to DEAL. He wore a number of labels. He had been assessed as having cerebral palsy, and attended the cerebral palsy clinic at the Children's Hospital, but had been rejected as a student by the cerebral palsy school on the grounds that he didn't have it. Whether or not he had cerebral palsy, it was obvious that he had significant neuromotor impairments—he had difficulty walking, and an unusual gait. He had also been assessed as severely intellectually impaired, and was attending a special school for children with IQs under 50. He had not been formally diagnosed as autistic, but he had a number of autistic traits—he was obsessed by electric lights, gazing at them and making stereotypic movements with his fingers, he rocked back and forth, and his attempts at speech were unclear but very repetitive. Ian's noises and rocking were certainly not the behavior of a typical 11-year-old and contributed to an impression of retardation, but these behaviors were offset by his sense of humor and his response to social situations. He was often the first person in the room to laugh at a joke.

Ian had very little functional speech. Very occasionally he was able to get out a clear sentence, but most of the time his speech was unintelligible, only the odd phrase or single word coming through. He had been involved in a manual signing program and could recognize 50 or more signs, but he did not produce anything like this many himself. He had been working with a speech therapist on word recognition, and over the years his mother had done much work with flash cards.

My notes from his first session in May 1986, read

> Ian is very distractible. He was fascinated by the light shade,
> which was the same as one he had at home, and in conse-
> quence we worked most of the time with the light off. Once
> having made eye contact, my eyes and face engrossed and
> amused him and it was often necessary for me to avert my
> eyes to get him back on task. Unless major efforts are made
> to get and keep Ian on task he will point randomly without
> looking, leading to a high error rate. If Ian is prevented from
> pointing until he is on task, his error rate drops markedly.

Ian had a habit of forcing eye contact—he would make a noise,
you'd look, he'd push his face up to yours and almost grab your
eyes with his. It was a mistake, I found, to turn to him when he
vocalized, and I found that deliberate eye avoidance until he was
back on task worked much better. Ian used this strategy very effectively to avoid tasks and to get attention. His concentration was also
interrupted by his frequent attempts to speak, which generally con-
sisted of the same phrases—"I will . . ." or "I would like . . ." taper-
ing off into incomprehensibility.

Ian demonstrated the use of his wordbook with his speech therapist without much enthusiasm. The wordbook had five words to a
page, and if Ian was asked to point to a named word he did so correctly 50% of the time. I put some word cards out in pairs. When I
held Ian's left wrist to keep him on task and to prevent his stereotypic hand movements he used his right hand to point to the nominated word from each pair with 100% success.

Ian's performance on word recognition was pleasing—for a person assessed as having severe mental retardation, he was doing
very well—but it did not lead me to question his diagnosis. Up to
this time DEAL had been working largely with people with severe
physical impairments, and Ian was one of the first children we had
seen who was able to walk. His physical skills seemed relatively
well developed—well developed, at least, for a child diagnosed as
having cerebral palsy—and if he was intellectually able to do something, such as recognize signs, then there appeared to be no physical reason why he could not make use of that knowledge. We had
not yet appreciated the significant effect motor planning problems
could have on the performance of people with developmental disabilities. My comments at the end of his first session were

> Ian's present communication program seems most appropriate. . . . In addition to direct communication benefits it may provide motivation for Ian to come to grips with some of his unproductive behavior and show more of his abilities, which may be greater than those he is using currently.

Ian did not come back to DEAL for 6 months. During that time, we had seen many more people like him—people with little or no functional speech who had been diagnosed as having significant intellectual impairments, who could walk, but who nonetheless had hand function impairments that prevented them from demonstrating all their skills. We were thinking about apraxia, and we were learning not to restrict the options offered to individuals because of the labels they wore. As a result, we had developed a different and more open-ended assessment strategy. It was based around a children's toy, a talking computer. The therapist presented a series of questions, spoken by the machine, which the student could answer by pressing the correct item on the display. On this session I supported Ian's right wrist. His index-finger pointing was fine, and in fact once his wrist was supported he had excellent hand and finger movement. You could hold him in one position and if the area to be covered was small he would swing his whole hand or finger to the key or item that he wanted. He completed the color sheet on the Talking Computer, where the machine asked him "Show me the word blue" or "Show me brown," and the picture sheet, where it asked "Show me the car" or "Show me the word house." On the sheet that had letters of the alphabet he was able to point correctly to the letters that I named. I asked him if he had anything he wanted to try and spell. He spelled I CANT FINCD LETTERS—which wasn't really true, although he had had to peer down and hunt around a bit to find them. He then spelled IL WRITE and IM IDIOTICK.

I then brought over a Canon Communicator, a mini-typewriter, which had a plastic guard over the letters that made it impossible to hit two letters at once, helping Ian to be both more accurate and more independent. I asked Ian about the way he kept saying "I will . . ." or "I would like . . ." and asked him to type what he wanted. He didn't, and the repeated phrases did not appear to indicate an actual need. I asked him why he was saying this if he didn't in fact want anything, and he typed I SPEEK SO YOU DON'T.

On his next visit Ian spelled with a volunteer holding his wrist, and on the visit after that, a speech therapist. Some of his spelling was phonetic, particularly of unusual words he may not have seen written down—rhinoceros, for example, was RINCEROS, which was a good attempt. His mother asked him to tell the therapist the name of a friend's dog, which was a check both on his memory and his ability to get out something that the therapist didn't know. Ian spelled BO: the dog's name was Beau. Shortly afterwards Ian started spelling to his mother, communicating with her as fluently as he did with any of the DEAL staff.

Ian's mother was frustrated with Ian's situation at the special school, where the staff appeared unwilling to undertake any communication programs, and had applied for him to attend a regular primary school for a couple of half-days a week in 1987. If he went to a regular school not only would he have the other children to model his language on, but while he was there he would have a one-on-one integration aid to work on his signing and his communication. This had all been set up before there was any thought of Ian communicating by spelling, and he spelled his first words just before he was due to start at his new school. At the beginning Ian was very noisy in the regular classroom, it was difficult to get him to do things, people really didn't know what level to address him at, and he was initially perceived very negatively. In particular, Ian had a problem with bursts of laughter. They were quite disruptive at DEAL, and must have been very disruptive in the classroom. I was never sure if they were involuntary or whether they were intentionally attention-seeking or disruptive.

Ian had been placed in fifth grade, and so was about 2 years older than the other children, but because of his relatively slight build didn't stand out as significantly different. His classroom behavior was a major problem and at first led to his being given very simple activities that were well below the level of the activities being done by the other children and well below his own ability level. He badly needed to communicate.

Six weeks after he had started at primary school his teacher and his integration aide came to DEAL and we arranged to teach the aide Ian's communication strategies. In a few weeks Ian had achieved fluency in spelling with his aide providing wrist support. It was soon possible to start fading support, and shortly he was able to spell with his facilitator's hand under his elbow. A speech therapist asked Ian what should be done about the noisy laughing. He spelled IF I KEEP LAUGHING TELL ME "KEEP QUIET"—VERY POLITELY. Laughter continued to be an issue for a while yet, and a month or so later Ian spelled out I AM A FOOL SO I DONT HAVE

TO DO ANY WORK. As Ian started demonstrating his real ability level his behavior in the classroom began to improve, and the amount of time that he was attending regular school was increased.

Many of DEAL's clients had neuromotor problems that were not necessarily apparent to the untrained eye, but in Ian's case his difficulties in walking had at least alerted everyone to the fact that he did have a genuine neuromotor problem and there was acceptance of the fact that he would need continuing physical and occupational therapy help. In June the school physiotherapist came and compared notes with our physiotherapist. Our physiotherapist hypothesized that some of Ian's rocking or stereotyped behaviors might be an attempt to achieve more proprioceptive feedback, and she tried standing behind Ian and pressing down firmly with her hands on his shoulders while he was typing. While he didn't like it, he spelled more fluently and quickly when given this strong proprioceptive input. The physiotherapist also commented on his poor eye fixation and tracking, his undeveloped hand function, and his general apraxia. It was decided to incorporate coactive bilateral or unilateral hand function tasks and more proprioceptive stimulus into his ongoing physiotherapy program, which would have been fine if Ian had been cooperative, which most of the time he wasn't.

By this time Ian was attending the primary school for five mornings and one afternoon a week. He was doing regular classroom work, and had reached this standard in ten weeks. He did have catch-up lessons in math twice a week, but obviously it wasn't a matter of him learning everything as he went; what was happening was that Ian's new ability to use a keyboard was allowing him to demonstrate language and reading skills that he already had.

While other DEAL staff continued to work with Ian I didn't see him again until September 1987, when I was brought in to read him the riot act because he wasn't doing much work at school. He was quite sensible throughout the session—no giggling or laughing, and only a couple of attempts at irrelevant speech. His eye contact was normal. Increasing Ian's independence was a priority; I found that Ian was able to do some spelling on the communicator without arm support but with firm pressure from my hands on his shoulders to provide proprioceptive input. This was successful for a short time, but three problems were obvious. First, he had difficulties lifting his arm against gravity and maintaining it in position against gravity, as he needed to do if he was to access the keyboard with one finger. Second, his forearm tended to roll outward leading to his thumb and index finger swinging up and away from the keyboard, so he might be pointing at a key but not be able to apply any pressure to it. This external rotation had been corrected by Ian's facilitators without the facilitators even realizing that they were doing this. Third, his wrist tended to bend, resulting in his hand dropping and his forefinger bending and, again, a difficulty in applying pressure, so that he might be hitting the right keys but not hard enough and his typing would come out with every second letter missing. When Ian's arm was supported, either at the elbow or by holding on to his sleeve, his forearm and wrist position normalized. This gave him stronger and easier finger movement. I tried sitting next to Ian and raising my knee so he could rest his arm across my knee as he was typing. That was quite effective, but there were going to be obvious difficulties using this method in the classroom. There didn't seem to be an immediate simple answer. We suggested various activities, such as poking holes in lumps of clay, that Ian could do to improve muscle tone in his finger, and others, such as lifting weights, that he could do to improve his overall arm and shoulder strength. These, and continued typing practice, produced some improvement.

By the end of his first year of spelling and typing Ian could type with just the touch of the facilitator's finger on his shoulder (and it wasn't clear why he even needed that) providing his communication aid was on a table that was lower than the armrest on his chair so he didn't have to lift his arm against gravity. When he had this little support, however, he was slower, and he couldn't sustain the effort for very long. Furthermore, independence reduced the accuracy of his pointing, and that meant he had to use larger squares for the letters. The only portable aid we had with letters this size was an early speech synthesizer, the Vocaid, which had letters about 2 cm square but had no written output and so while perfectly adequate for social conversations was useless for producing schoolwork. Ian himself said that he preferred being held—LESS ARM SUPPORT IS HARD WITH ARM SUPPORT I FEEL BETTER.

In 1988 Ian was a full-time student in Grade 6 in a regular primary school. DEAL continued to work with him and to provide information and training to his teachers and aides. He was seen by our occupational therapist to assess his hand function and to advise him on the best keyboard for him to use. She commented on the difficulty that Ian had with praxis—with getting the correct movement to happen. The attempt was clearly there, but the execution was flawed. Ian scored 37/75 on the Upper Extremity Function Test with his right hand (his dominant hand). Our technician started to design a chair especially for him with an adjustable armrest for arm support and a stand for the communication aid.

By this time there was disquiet among some professionals in Victoria at the results that were being achieved by Ian and other people with similar diagnoses who were attending DEAL. As a result a government agency, the Intellectual Disability Review Panel (IDRP), was asked to conduct an official inquiry into what they called "assisted communication." Ian was concerned that DEAL was under threat, and in August he typed a message for the DEAL Annual General Meeting.

> A chance to communicate is ever so important.
> You should never deny someone the opportunity
> to talk. I think that my life is just start-
> ing to come together now. I hate having peo-
> ple doubt that I can understand, but it is so
> hard not to behave as if I was stupid.

The Panel tested 6 DEAL clients in the latter part of 1988. Ian was one of them. By this stage Ian had been facilitated by numerous staff, aides, and family members, and he typed successfully with one of the investigators facilitating him. The test he was given to confirm that he rather than his facilitator originated the typing was simple, quick and straightforward. The investigators gave Ian a present while his regular facilitator was absent—a book called *The Man From Snowy River* containing a well known nineteenth-century Australian poem about a stockman rounding up wild horses. When the facilitator was called back into the room he had to tell her what he had been given. Ian typed "BOOK." Asked what the book was about, he typed "EARLY DAYS." The investigators' conclusion was that

> It is clear from the above message passing exercise that this client's communication whilst using assisted communication has been confirmed. (*Intellectual Disability Review Panel*, 1989, p.38)

Overall, four of the six DEAL clients tested by the IDRP validated their communication using facilitation.

With increased typing fluency Ian's sense of humor started showing itself in creative writing. Near the end of 1988 he entered a competition conducted by Telecom, the Australian Government telephone company, for a piece of writing about telephones. The competition was open to anyone, adult or child, and Ian won a prize with a quirky poem that satisfied Telecom's needs perfectly.

```
I'm in the bath midst clouds of steam
enveloped in a rosy dream.
Ring! Ring! O dreaded sound I hear
And dripping wet, a towel I wear.
"Do you know the price of gold?"
Wrong number! Now the water's cold.
```

Ironically, because of Ian's speech impairments he himself had never been able to use a telephone.

In 1989 our technician completed Ian's specially adapted chair. It certainly worked in one way—using it Ian was able to type more independently, needing only his facilitator's hand on his shoulder— but in that year Ian started secondary school, and instead of being in the same classroom all day he had to move between classrooms. Ian's weak shoulders and poor balance precluded him from carrying anything substantial; his aide already had to carry a bag of books and a typewriter between classes, and carrying a chair as well was obviously impractical. We tried a detachable armrest, to be used with the school chairs, but even that was too much. In any case, secondary school demanded such quantities of written work that to some extent independence had to be sacrificed to speed. Provided the keyboard was low enough Ian could by this stage type with just a facilitator's touch on his head; indeed, he could type briefly with no contact at all. However, this was very slow. If he had support at the elbow his output was much faster. Ian not only had to do the same amount of homework as the other children, only more slowly, but also had to catch up after school on any work he hadn't completed in the classroom. Greater independence with less speed could mean he would have 4 hours work every evening, and he was only in seventh grade.

When Ian first started at secondary school all the students were asked to draw pictures of themselves. Because Ian didn't have the hand skills to draw a picture, he wrote it.

ME

```
This is a portrait of strange me.
I cannot draw, so you can see
I'll have to paint it all in words.
My eyes are blue, my hair is fair,
My type of speaking is quite rare,
A skinny weed I seem to be.
Inside I am a man of dreams -
```

```
Of fearless deeds and cunning schemes,
A handsome superman
In fact, when in a pensive mood,
I'm better far than Robin Hood
Or even Sherlock Holmes.
I'm Liberace on the keys
And white Shark Norman on the tees,
Jack Brabham in the car.
So when you meet me at the school
I may be Armstrong in the pool -
So look out for the
                              SPLASH!
```

Norman, Brabham, and Armstrong are Australian sporting heroes.

By this stage DEAL's involvement with Ian was limited to training his new integration teacher and integration aides, and occasional troubleshooting. Ian had gradually become quieter in the primary school classroom, but his noises and inappropriate laughter reappeared when he started secondary school. While he was able to type quite fluently to his new aides, Ian was not doing much work in the classroom, and one of our speech therapists went down to his school to observe him. She felt that one of the reasons for his lack of cooperation was that he couldn't do some of the work, and she instituted detailed language testing. It appeared that Ian had some difficulty with reading, in part relating to visual coordination problems and in part to visual acuity. Ian got glasses shortly afterwards and his problems improved significantly. He also showed some minor difficulties with short-term memory and word retrieval, and some difficulties with decoding some complex language structures. These problems had affected Ian's ability to perform in the classroom. The speech therapist asked Ian about it. He said there had been a problem, that he hadn't told anyone about it because he felt he would be excluded from the school, and he didn't want her telling anyone either. There was in fact no risk of exclusion and Ian was doing well with the work that he did do. DEAL recommended some changes in the way work was presented to Ian—that printed material be enlarged on the photocopier, that distracting peripheral material be removed, that he be given help in following along the line when reading either by having other lines screened or by having a ruler below the line he was looking at. The problems gradually resolved, or perhaps more accurately accommodations were found.

In 1990 Ian won a certificate of distinction in a schools science competition for eighth grade students all over Australia. His academic work was perfectly satisfactory, but other problems were pushing themselves to the fore. Ian was older than the other students in the class, because he'd started at regular school much later. His classmates were 13 going on 14, hitting puberty and becoming very conscious of Ian's differences, and Ian, now 16, was also increasingly aware of the things that the other students were doing and he was missing out on. At the end of the year Ian wrote a follow-up to his earlier self-portrait.

Daydreaming

```
Sixteen years of super dreams
Have faded to reality -
No longer images of fame
Drift through my personality.
Once I loved to sit alone,
Dreaming I was flying high
Taking capsules to the moon,
Fighting Rambo! Now I sigh.
Each day I was like a super scout,
Making the world a better place,
Playing tennis just like Cash
In every game I held the ace.
Cached in my mind, a mighty fund
Of stories with myself as hero -
Now at last the sad truth dawns;
Down my hopes have gone to zero.
Here I am, a weakling lad.
What replaces all my dreams?
Earthbound, speechless, without friends,
A teenage misfit in blue jeans.
```

At around this time his diagnoses were reviewed. His pediatrician diagnosed him as autistic, and the label of intellectual impairment was removed. People with autism are sometimes said to be unable to understand human relationships, but Ian seems to have a grasp of them at about the level of his peers. In 1992 he wrote about his very nice sister.

```
My sister broke up with her boyfriend last
week and she is a real pain since then. I like
Tommy living with us, sometimes he would play
```

```
ball with me and I sit and watch him do his
drawings. My sister is a fool and lazy, all
she cares about is herself and her ugly dogs.
I wish she would like me better, she hates me
I think. I wish she would take me out for a
drive sometimes in her nice car and meet her
friends.
```

My Sister

```
My sister is a fool.
Just as silly as her dogs.
Poor old Tommy got thrown out the other day
  to his dismay.
I miss him terribly. At least he was sane.
As for the dogs they could have gone too.
Oh listen to Lisa weep.
But why? She threw him out.
Oh God I wish she'd get married and move
  away.
That's my sister. Crazy —
Doesn't even know when she had it good.
```

The Victorian Certificate of Education, the final assessment for
secondary school students, extends over 2 years, and Ian will take
at least 3 years. He is about to conclude his 1st year (1993). Because
of the quantity of work involved, he is able to do only a small number of subjects, but his results to date are quite satisfactory, despite
some difficulty in getting up to speed with a new aide.

As speed is of paramount importance at this level, independent
typing is again taking a back seat. Despite having a lot of occupational therapy input over the past few years, Ian is still very significantly slower if he types alone or with less than elbow support. Perhaps if he had started working on typing and arm and hand
function much younger, he would now be able to type independently at a reasonable speed.

Subjectively there appears to have been an increase in the
number of appropriate spoken responses Ian makes. Certainly
there has been a significant diminution of inappropriate speech,
noises, and giggling, though all can still recur, along with his stereotyped hand flapping, if Ian is excited or tense. Ian's eye contact is
good, and he uses nonspeech gestures such as shaking hands or giving five appropriately.

Ian's story illustrates the value of a multidisciplinary approach to nonspeech communication. He required input from almost every team member and from every discipline. His development parallels the development of facilitated communication training at DEAL, in that Ian was one of the clients we learnt from and practiced on. The challenges for the future are for Ian to find a satisfying role after he finishes school, and for us to find a way for him to access an appropriate communication aid quickly and independently. A small laptop with word completion and prediction strategies and voice output may offer him most in terms of empowerment.

CASE STUDY 2—PAUL

Paul was 12 years old and in sixth grade at his neighborhood school when he was brought to the communication center by his parents in September 1989. His parents were in their 40s and had professional qualifications. Paul was the second of their three children. He has Down syndrome.

Paul's gross motor development was only mildly delayed and he walked alone at 18 months. He said his first word at 18 months and his first two and three word utterances at 24 months. As a toddler, Paul's speech varied from day to day, and this pattern continued through his primary school years. Sometimes he spoke in sentences and initiated conversations. On other occasions he seemed to have difficulty giving one word answers to questions. Paul had speech/language therapy for an hour a week for 2 years between the ages of 6 and 8, when all therapy was discontinued because of lack of progress. At age 12, Paul would occasionally utter a complex sentence; more commonly he would use two or three word utterances, and sometimes he wouldn't even manage that, responding to questions not at all or with gestures. While Paul had some articulation problems his speech was generally intelligible. To some extent his speech appeared to reflect his muscle tone, which was variable. On days when Paul's body almost seemed too heavy for him to move, his speech was more limited and less clear, and he didn't initiate conversation or movement. On days when he was full of energy, his muscle tone was higher and he spoke far more. While his oral language still wasn't normal, and he still couldn't say everything he wanted to say, which frustrated him, he could speak when he was spoken to and he would spontaneously ask questions and make comments, displaying a wicked sense of humor. However, even when he was at his most vocal, his responses to complex instructions and to jokes on subjects such as politics indicated that his comprehension was well in advance of his speech production

One extra problem plagued Paul and his family. He would perseverate and say the same word again and again. "Banana" had been the first word he'd said at kindergarten, and had been much praised. Encouraged, he said it so often that it became automatic and came out at all kinds of inappropriate moments. Paul was not beyond using "banana" deliberately to stir his parents; unfortunately, every time he did so made it more likely that it would come out when not wanted.

Paul had done a modified school curriculum at the local primary school. He sat in with the class, but he wasn't expected to do everything they did. At age 12 he had writing skills at about a 6- or 7-year-old level. His writing showed motor planning and perseveration problems. He could not read aloud but he spent a lot of time turning the pages of age-appropriate books. His family watched him with amusement and thought that he was imitating his sisters. His mother said that he could play the piano a little as a result of long-term teaching, but had difficulty tying his shoelaces. He was independent and walked to and from school by himself.

Paul was due to start at secondary school in February of 1990. His parents and teachers were concerned as to how he would cope both socially and academically in his new school and were seeking help with his communication. At this stage, his parents were looking for augmentative strategies that could help Paul make himself understood. It had been suggested that Paul use Australasian Deaf Sign. (In Victoria the Makaton sign vocabulary [Grove & Walker, 1990] is probably the augmentative strategy most commonly used with people with Down syndrome [Iacono & Parsons, 1986]). However, several important considerations had been overlooked. Communication partners fluent in sign were not available in a regular secondary school. While it is possible in a primary school to teach sign to the signing student's class and teacher this is more difficult at secondary level, where the student moves from class to class. Also, it was difficult to answer schoolwork-related questions in a restricted sign vocabulary, and the signing required certain motor skills (Klein, 1982). When asked to imitate a simple hand posture, holding up both hands with the index fingers extended and the other fingers flexed, Paul was unable to do so and had to use his left hand to hold down the fingers of his right hand to achieve index finger isolation. This did not mean sign acquisition would be impossible, but it did raise significant questions about the ease with which Paul would be able to learn sign shapes.

Like most older children and adults I have seen with severe communication impairments associated with a diagnosis of intellectual impairment, Paul appeared to suffer from a lack of self-confidence. When spoken to, he hung his head and "went blank" or feigned deafness. Initially he made no apparent effort to do anything I asked. He was sullen and uncooperative until offered a toy, My Talking Computer, which had a voice. My initial assessment was based around this toy, which can be used to ask questions that explore the student's knowledge of concepts from picture recognition to composing sentences by selecting written words. After successfully completing all the assigned tasks Paul typed his name, and typed I CAN READ I GET SILLY I CANT STOP SOMETIMES SCHOOL THINK I'M STUPID on a Communicator. He had considerable difficulty isolating an index finger to hit the letters. This was remedied by having him hold a rod in his palm with his other fingers. Paul's communication partner held the other end of the rod to compensate for his low muscle tone and endurance (and to stop him from fooling around). Testing showed reading comprehension appropriate for his age. This is not exceptional; Buckley (1985) cites a number of examples of children with Down syndrome who had reading comprehension skills equal to or in advance of their age peers. Paul's spelling was poor but his vocabulary appeared to be above average and he used standard syntax.

Paul had a bad habit of regressing to immature behavior whenever he felt anxious. Whether he felt anxious because he was in a new situation or because people were in fact babying him, the behavior was unproductive. Toward the end of 1989 Paul paid a number of visits to his future secondary school. His behavior was inappropriate. When asked to do things he laid down on the floor and refused to budge, he said "banana" a lot, and he demonstrated few skills.

Over the 6 weeks of the Christmas holidays Paul communicated fluently with all of his immediate family by typing on a Communicator. In that time he used the Communicator everywhere he went, with his extended family, with neighbors, and with friends. He was reported as walking taller, looking people in the face, and responding, orally or on the Communicator, when spoken to. Paul attributed the change to his new means of communication. His family reported that they started to interact with him differently as he showed them unexpected capabilities and understanding through his typing.

By July, 1990 Paul's new teacher, who had been dreading his arrival, was able to say, "Now he's just another kid." His contact with the communication center was limited to monthly communication groups in which he had no hesitation in expressing his opinion: "I INSIST ON ACADEMIC [WORK] ON THE NEXT SESSION BEING HELD HERE AND AM I DAMN WELL GOING TO GET IT." He no longer had a modified syllabus. In December 1990 his best examination result was 90% in German, which was a new subject for all the students. He could type short answers without any facilitation, but he tired quickly. In most classes he was accompanied by an integration aide. If she was not there and he needed someone to hold the end of the rod when he was typing longer answers, he just asked one of the other students to help. In 1991 his mother and teacher reported that Paul was speaking more and that his spoken vocabulary had increased. Clunies-Ross (1990) found that the reading skills of young children with Down syndrome could be used to improve their understanding and use of spoken language. Paul generally introduced new words into his oral system after he had typed them, though he certainly has not said every word he has typed, and he still has problems reading aloud. A speech/language pathologist has recently suggested that he has significant oral dyspraxia.

By 1991 Paul no longer had problems with index finger isolation and his tendency to perseverate on selections had abated. Consequently it was possible to administer a Peabody Picture Vocabulary Test—Form M (Dunn & Dunn, 1981) with no facilitation. To ensure scanning, each of the four plates was indicated by the examiner before the question was asked, and Paul was encouraged to pause before responding. His score was above the 99th percentile, confirming the initial impression that Paul had an excellent vocabulary.

Paul's communication training continues in 1993. He needs to become fully independent in typing, to augment both his speech and his handwriting. He also needs quick ways of getting across routine messages such as lunch orders on days when his speech lets him down. Communication wallets containing words and phrases specific to different situations need to be developed. Paul also has to learn to select the appropriate communication strategy for each situation, out of speech, gesture, communication wallet, and typing. The need to select the appropriate mode became obvious when Paul, in midadolescence, started swearing at his aides on the Communicator. As the evidence was incontrovertible, he was frequently suspended from school. If he had sworn in speech, he might have gotten away with it.

THE CHALLENGE

Ian and Paul are two individuals with severe communication impairments who had been judged to be respectively severely and moderately intellectually impaired. Training in nonspeech communication has enabled both of them to challenge the labels they had been given. Each had different hand function impairments that affected his ability to use augmentative communication, and each used facilitation to circumvent these impairments. For communication training to be successful it was as necessary to examine and treat hand function as it was to assess speech/language. Their experiences suggest that individuals who have both severely impaired oral language and impaired hand function are especially vulnerable to misassessment of their intellectual functioning.

The achievements of Paul and other students with Down syndrome who have been given alternatives to speech and writing add to the considerable body of literature drawing attention to "unexpected" achievements by individuals with Down syndrome.(Clunies-Ross, 1986). To date, it has been assumed that, while there may have been an overall underestimation of the potential of individuals with Down syndrome, only a small group of "higher functioning" individuals have normal, or borderline, intelligence. This small group may consist of those individuals who have unimpaired, or less severely affected, speech and fine motor skills, thus enabling them to attack standardized tests more successfully. This could parallel the earlier experience of another diagnostic group, individuals with cerebral palsy.

Sixty years ago the received wisdom was that the severity of the physical impairment in cerebral palsy mirrored the severity of the intellectual impairment. Now, with the advent of electronic communication and mobility aids, it has become clear that there is no necessary correlation between the severity of the physical impairment and intellectual status. Many individuals with cerebral palsy without intelligible speech or functional hand skills have successfully completed college. Whether such academic achievements are possible for any individuals with Down syndrome cannot be known with certainty until the first group of students who have had their expressive impairments addressed from infancy has proceeded through the regular school system.

Because Ian and Paul are ambulatory, they needed easily portable communication aids that they could access with their hands. Facilitated communication training has provided them with a means of communication while they develop the necessary accessing skills. Other DEAL clients who initially required similar levels of facilitation are now typing independently, and this remains the goal for Ian and Paul. Until they are independent their ability to communicate, and the influence exerted by their facilitators, may be questioned (IDRP, 1989).

Johnson (1989) and Biklen and Schubert (1991) describe the use of similar facilitation techniques for similar reasons by children and adults assessed as intellectually impaired and/or autistic in Denmark and the United States. The incidence of treatable fine motor problems and speech/language impairments in older children and adults will presumably be less in localities where all preschoolers with development disabilities are given thorough neuromotor screening and have access to remedial programs. Even with the best of early intervention programs there will still be children with severe communication impairments requiring augmentative communication; however, concentration on the preliminary skills needed for manual signing and aid access, together with a positive attitude toward the potential of children with severe communication impairments, would significantly reduce the need for facilitated communication training.

The outcomes of individuals using facilitated communication suggest that further research is needed in many areas: the nature of the association between impairments of oral language and fine motor skills; the adequacy of the intellectual assessment of children with severe communication impairments; the incidence of remediable neuromotor problems in individuals assessed as intellectually impaired, and the informal acquisition of literacy skills through environmental exposure. Lastly, many questions directly concerned with the facilitation process need investigation.

Ian and Paul had one thing in common. Their lives were at stages where it was impossible to put their communication on hold while lengthy training programs were implemented, even if the resources had been available to mount such programs (Beukelman, 1991). Haney (1988) proposes a 5- to 6-year time frame, starting from the initial augmentative communication intervention, for the achievement of communication competence, with aid use *commencing* in the 3rd and 4th years. Facilitated communication training is not an ideal solution to severe communication problems, but these individuals do not present ideal problems. Despite its obvious limitations and disadvantages facilitated communication training did enable these individuals to achieve goals previously thought to be impossible. It is a teaching strategy that should be considered for individuals with severe communication impairments whose hand skills limit their ability to use communication aids successfully. As Anne McDonald said (Crossley & McDonald, 1984, p. 76), "Unless someone makes a jump by going outside the handicapped person's previous stage of communication, there is no way the speechless person can do so. Failure is no crime. Failure to give someone the benefit of the doubt is."

Appendix A
Terminology

—•— ⟫⟪ —•—

COMMUNICATION

COMMUNICATION: Sharing of ideas and information using a mutually known system. For example, you can communicate with a deaf person who uses sign language if you also know sign language.

AIDED COMMUNICATION: Any communication strategy requiring the use of a communication aid. Speech, gesture and manual sign are all UNAIDED communication strategies.

ALTERNATIVE COMMUNICATION: Forms of communication (such as signing, using communication boards or devices) used instead of speech when speech is nonexistent or unintelligible.

ASSISTED COMMUNICATION: Communication by a person in which the response of that person is expressed through the use of equipment and is dependent upon the assistance of another person, e.g., a person using an eye-pointing board needs the assistance of a partner, who has to observe and translate the user's eye movements.

AUGMENTATIVE COMMUNICATION: Forms of communication that augment, or add to speech, e.g., Jane's speech is understood by her family but not by strangers so when she is out and about she augments her speech by using a communication book.

COMMUNICATION FRUSTRATION: Negative behavior arising from an inability to communicate or an inability to communicate as one would wish, e.g., when the word required cannot be found on a communication display.

FACILITATED COMMUNICATION: An assistive communication technique in which the primary message receiver makes physical contact with the sender to help them overcome motor or emotional problems, e.g., poor muscle tone, lack of confidence. It

131

differs from coactive movement in that the direction of movement and intention to complete an action are solely the responsibility of the message sender. Facilitation is mainly used when training people to use communication aids.

NONVERBAL COMMUNICATION: Nonverbal means not involving words, e.g., gesture. It is often incorrectly used as meaning without speech, for which the appropriate terms are nonspeech or nonoral. People who type but do not talk are not nonverbal, but nonspeaking.

COMMUNICATION AID USE

ACCESS: Means of using a communication aid, e.g., finger pointing, head pointing. Access is split into two types:

DIRECT ACCESS: Includes any aid usage in which the communication aid user directly indicates the items they want, e.g., by eye pointing, fist pointing, and so forth.

INDIRECT ACCESS: Involves scanning. Items on a communication display are indicated in turn, either manually by a partner or electronically by a light or a cursor. The communication aid user stops the scanner when the item they want is reached, either by signalling or by hitting a switch.

DEDICATED DEVICE: A piece of communication equipment designed for use by people with severe communication impairments, and not used by people without disabilities, e.g., Canon Communicator, Wolf, All-talk. Typewriters, pocket computers, and regular computers are not dedicated devices; they are used in many ways by the community at large.

DISPLAY: Any set of items from which a communication aid user chooses, e.g., a communication board with 6 pictures on it, a combined symbol/word board, or a computer screen with words and letters.

FADING: Gradually reducing the amount of facilitation provided to a communication aid user, e.g., support may be faded from wrist to elbow to shoulder before being withdrawn entirely.

PHONETIC SPELLING: Spelling words as they sound, for example:

ornj = orange.

jon u shood cum to skool = John you should come to school.

Sometimes aid users use letters to represent similar sounding words, for example:

RUOK = are you okay

WORD PREDICTION: "On Tuesd__ I wa__ ver__ sa__ becau__ my pet do__ die__ ." Often when a communication aid user is spelling you can fill in the whole word. Many computerized communication aids use similar word prediction strategies to speed up message production. Most aid users appreciate it if their partners say the whole word when the ending is obvious, thus saving time and allowing the aid user to go on to the next word. If your guess is wrong, the aid user will continue spelling the word, ignoring your wrong attempt.

NEUROMOTOR IMPAIRMENTS

NEUROMOTEOR IMPAIRMENTS: Problems with producing desired movement patterns (e.g., speech) due to neurological dysfunction (e.g., brain damage).

EYE/HAND COORDINATION: The ability to coordinate eye and hand movements. In the simplest sense, the ability to keep your eyes on what you're doing. More complex aspects include correlating perception of depth and strength of movement.

INHIBITION: Stopping unnecessary or inappropriate movements, e.g., we inhibit ourselves from scratching our noses when being photographed. To make controlled, voluntary, movements it is necessary to inhibit involuntary movement.

DISINHIBITION: Is the opposite of inhibition. Many people with poor eye/hand coordination are visually disinhibited—that is, they are unable to inhibit the automatic movement of their eyes to anything in their environment that moves or makes a noise.

INITIATION PROBLEMS: Difficulty in starting a movement, even though the person wants to move. People with initiation problems may need a spoken or physical prompt to start moving, e.g., a tap on the elbow to start typing.

Muscle tone: The state of the muscle that allows natural movement. Some people's muscle tone is too low **(hypotonia)**: their limbs feel floppy and heavy. Some people's muscle tone is too high **(hypertonia)**: their muscles feel tight and their limbs feel stiff.

Perseveration: Movements or actions are repeated more than is necessary or appropriate. There can be perseveration in speech "I went to the shops, shops, went to the shops to shops to buy shops." There can be perseveration in written words "I am in in inside in my class." Sometimes perseveration of a sequence will cue another unwanted word as in the above example of *in* and *inside*. Sometimes a typist cannot get as far as a word—they get stuck on the first letter and hit it again and again, or they hit the correct letter then every other letter in the row.

SPEECH IMPAIRMENTS

Aphasia: Loss or impairment of the ability to use words or sounds.

Receptive (Wernicke's) **aphasia:** Affects the ability to decode spoken and/or written language. It is less common than expressive aphasia (which it may accompany).

Expressive (Broca's) **aphasia:** Affects the ability to speak and/or write. There may be problems with recall of words, confusion between words with similar sounds (e.g., saying "knife" for "life"), or difficulty in repeating something just heard.

Apraxia (also referred to as **Dyspraxia**): A neurological condition that prevents a person from routinely reproducing voluntary muscle movements. A person who has this condition may be able to reproduce the same movements spontaneously or involuntarily. (This distinguishes oral dyspraxia from dysarthria, as in the latter there is a motor deficit in *both* voluntary and involuntary speech.) A person with severe oral apraxia is often said, quite incorrectly, to be able to "speak when he wants to" because he has been heard to speak in the past. In fact, what he said may have been **involuntary** (e.g., swear words), **automatic** (e.g., completions, such as "Shut the—"), or **spontaneous** (e.g., greetings) and it's precisely **voluntary speech** that he is unable to produce, that is, he *cannot* talk when he wants to.

DYSARTHRIA: An impairment in the functioning of the musculature of respiration, phonation and articulation due to a lesion in the peripheral nervous system, central nervous system or both. Involvement of muscle groups controlling the tongue, the palate, the vocal cords, and breathing can seriously affect the intelligibility of speech. Total lack of speech for this reason is called anarthria.

ECHOLALIA: The repetition of previously heard utterances exactly as heard. Echolalic speech is fairly commonly associated with other word-finding problems. Individuals with echolalia are often diagnosed as autistic.

WORD-FINDING PROBLEM: Frequent inability to find the correct word. We all experience occasional word finding difficulties: "Can you bring me the whatsit from the whosits?" For some individuals the problem is very severe and prevents functional communication. The effect is similar to expressive aphasia.

Appendix B
Common Hand Function Problems

POOR EYE-HAND COORDINATION: The student makes selections without looking, or without allowing enough time between movements to scan the display and locate the target.

LOW MUSCLE TONE: The student's arm and hand are "floppy" or "heavy." There is difficulty raising the arm against gravity and muscles fatigue quickly.

HIGH MUSCLE TONE: The student's arm feels tense, and their movements are often too forceful, either over-reaching the target or pushing the aid away.

INDEX FINGER ISOLATION AND EXTENSION PROBLEMS: The student has difficulty in extending a first finger while holding back the other fingers. Users with this problem either point with all fingers extended or use the middle finger (which is the longest). Either method makes accurate selection difficult.

PERSEVERATION: The student makes a selection and continues hitting either that selection or adjacent selections inappropriately.

USING BOTH HANDS FOR A TASK ONLY REQUIRING ONE: If a student points to two items simultaneously it is hard to be sure which item (if either) was actually desired.

TREMOR: Tremor can either be a continuous tremor or an intention tremor, where the hand is stable while at rest but trembles when the person tries to do something (such as point).

RADIAL/ULNAR MUSCLE INSTABILITY: The muscles of forearm, wrist, and hand exert unequal pull on the hand or fingers. Sometimes the index finger swerves to one side as the student goes to point, leading to unwanted selections. The most common problem is for the aid user's index finger to move across in front of the other fingers. Often the hand also drops down from the wrist thus making the tip of the index finger invisible to its owner, who is then pointing blind.

INITIATION PROBLEMS: The student does not spontaneously reach out to the communication display.

IMPULSIVITY: The student moves too fast to produce considered responses—starts pointing at the answer before you've finished the question, or points quickly all over the board so that you don't know which item was meant. .

PROXIMAL INSTABILITY: The person's whole arm moves from side to side. Often an overarm pointing action, rather than the more controlled underarm action, is used.

REDUCED PROPRIOCEPTION: The aid user has a reduced sense of body and arm position, affecting the accuracy of responses.

LACK OF CONFIDENCE: While not itself a physical problem, nervousness certainly affects physical performance.

Appendix C
Basic Principles of Facilitation

1. **MONITOR EYE CONTACT:** Check that the individual you are facilitating is looking at the communication display or keyboard. Developing eye-hand coordination and self-monitoring skills is essential if support is to be reduced.
2. **MONITOR OUTPUT:** Let the communication aid user know if you are not getting the message. If someone types a string of consonants with no vowels, encourage them to erase it and start over from the last intelligible item. Sometimes individuals produce rubbish when they are not sure what to say— perhaps the question needs clarification or the conversation needs more structure.
3. **PULL BACK:** Not one of the hand function problems listed above is assisted by pushing the aid user's hand forward. Many are helped by providing resistance, pulling back, or slowing down the aid user. A habit of pulling back or providing resistance protects facilitators against accidentally leading the aid user to an answer.
4. **REDUCE SUPPORT:** The aim of facilitated communication training is independent aid use. The amount of facilitation used should be reviewed frequently. It should always be the minimum needed for successful aid use.
5. **DON'T OVER-INTERPRET:** Be aware that any meaning you place on a string of consonants without a vowel or a string of nouns without a verb is your interpretation. "Mummy milk" may be easy to interpret accurately; "Man knife" is not.
6. **DON'T BELIEVE EVERYTHING YOU'RE TOLD:** People with disabilities are just as prone to exaggerate, fantasize, and lie as the rest of us. An inherently improbable statement does not become true just because it is typed.

References

Beukelman, D. R. (1991). Magic and cost of communication competence. *Augmentative and Alternative Communication, 1,* 2–10.

Biklen, D., & Schubert, A. (1991). New words: The communication of students with autism. *Remedial and Special Education, 12*(6), 47–57.

Bloomberg, K., & Johnson, H. (1990). A statewide demographic survey of people with severe communication impairments. *Augmentative and Alternative Communication, 1,* 50–60.

Buckley, S. (1985). Attaining basic educational skills: reading, writing and number. In D. Lane & B Stratford (Eds) *Current approaches to Down's syndrome* (pp 315–343). London: Holt, Rinehart and Winston.

Clunies-Ross, G. (1986). The development of children with Down's syndrome: Lessons from the past and implications for the future. *Australian Paediatric Journal, 22,* 167–169.

Clunies-Ross, G. (1990). Intellectual disability—language and reading. In *The right to read—Publishing for people with reading disabilities.* Canberra, Australia: National Library of Australia.

Cornforth, A. R. T., Johnson, K., & Walker, M. (1974) Makaton vocabulary: Teaching sign language to the deaf mentally handicapped, *Apex, 1,* 23–24.

Crossley, R., & McDonald, A. (1984). *Annie's coming out.* New York: Penguin-Viking.

Dumas, A. (1845). *The count of monte cristo.* trans. Lowell Blair 1956, New York: Bantam Books

Dunn, L., & Dunn, L. (1981). *Peabody Picture Vocabulary Test—Revised, Form M.* Circle Pines, MN: American Guidance Services.

Grove, N., & Walker, M. (1990). The Makaton Vocabulary; Using manual signs and graphic symbols to develop interpersonal communication. *Augmentative and Alternative Communication, 1, 15–28.*

Haney, C. (1988). Communication device today, competency tomorrow: Are we being realistic in our expectations. *Assistive Device News, 2,* 5–6.

Harrington, K. (1988). A letter from Annie. *Communicating Together, 4,* 5.

Iacono, T. A., & Parsons, C. L. (1986). A survey on the use of sign programmes in Victorian facilities for the intellectually disabled. *Australian Communication Quarterly, 2, 21–25.*

IDRP—Intellectual Disability Review Panel (1989). *Report to the Director General on the reliability and validity of assisted communication.* Melbourne, Australia: Office of Intellectual Disability Services.

Johnson, I. (1989). Hellish difficult to live in this world. *Journal of Social Work Practice, 1,* 13–29.

Klein, M. D. (1982*). Pre-Sign Language Motor Skills.* Tucson, AZ: Communication Skill Builders.

La Pointe, J. (1984). *Reading Comprehension Battery for Aphasia.* Tizard, OR: C.C. Publications.

McDonald, E. T., & Schultz, A. R. (1973). Communication boards for cerebral palsied children. *Journal of Speech and Hearing Disorders, 38,* 73–88.

McNaughton, S. (1990). Gaining the most from augmentative communication's growing years. *Augmentative and Alternative Communication,1,* 2–14.

McNaughton, S., & Kates, B. (1980). The application of Blissymbolics. In R.L. Schiefelbusch (ed) *Nonspeech language and communication; Analysis and intervention.* (pp 303–321), Baltimore: University Park Press.

Oppenheim, R. F. (1977). *Effective teaching methods for autistic children.* Springfield, IL: Charles C. Thomas.

Police v. Williams (1990, May). Moe Magistrates Court, Australia.

Sacks, O. (1989). *Seeing voices.* Berkeley and Los Angeles: University of California Press,

Vicker, B. (1974). *Non-oral communication system project. 1964–73, Iowa University Hospital School,:* University of Iowa.

Victorian Symbol Standardization Committee (1983). *COMPIC Computer Pictographs for Communication.* Melbourne, Australia: Swinburne Institute of Technology.

Bibliography

American Psychiatric Association (1980). *Diagnostic and statistical manual of mental disorders,* Third Edition. New York: Author.

Attwood, T. (1992). Movement disorders and autism: A rationale for the use of facilitated communication. *Communication, 26 (3),* 27.

Attwood, T., & Remington-Gurney, J. (1992). Assessment of literacy skill using facilitated communication. In C. Van Kraayenoord (Ed), *A survey of adult literacy provision for people with intellectual disabilities.* Brisbane, Schonell Special Education Research Centre, University of Queensland.

Berger, C. L. (1992). Facilitated communication: The breakthrough. *Communication Outlook, 14 (3),* 5.

Beukelman, D.R. (1991). Magic and cost of communication competence. *Augmentative and Alternative Communication, 1,* 2–10.

Beukelman, D., & Mirenda, P. (1992). *Augmentative and alternative communication: Management of severe communication disorders in children and adults.* Baltimore: Paul H. Brookes.

Biklen, D. (1990). Communication unbound: Autism and praxis. *Harvard Education Review, 60 (3),* 291.

Biklen, D. (1992). Typing to talk: Facilitated communication. *American Journal of Speech-Language Pathology, 1 (2),* 15.

Biklen, D. (1992). Autism orthodoxy versus free speech; A reply to Cummins and Prior. *Harvard Educational Review, 62 (2),* 242.

Biklen, D. (1992). Facilitated communication: Biklen responds. *American Journal of Speech-Language Pathology, 1 (2),* 21.

Biklen, D., & Schubert, A. (1991). New words: The communication of students with autism. *Remedial and Special Education, 12 (6),* 47.

Biklen, D., Morton, M., Saha, S., Duncan, J., Hardodottir, M., Karna, E., O'Connor, S., & Rao, S. (1991). I AMN NOT A UTISTIC OH THJE TYP (I am not autistic on the typewriter). *Disabilty, Handicap & Society, 6 (3),* 161.

Biklen, D., Morton, M., Gold, D., Berrigan, C., & Swaminathan, S. (1992). Facilitated communication: Implications for individuals with autism. *Topics in Language Disorders, 12 (4),* 1.

Calculator, S. (1992). Perhaps the emperor has clothes after all: A response to Biklen. *American Journal of Speech-Language Pathology, 1 (2),* 18.

Calculator, S., (1992). Facilitated communication: Calculator responds. *American Journal of Speech-Language Pathology, 1 (2),* 23.

Calculator, S., & Singer, K. (1992). Preliminary validation of facilitated communication. *Topics in Language Disorders, 12 (5),* ix.

Crossley, R. (1988). Unexpected communication attainments by persons diagnosed as autistic and intellectually impaired. Paper delivered at the Biennial ISAAC Conference, Anaheim, California, 1988.

Crossley, R. (1990). Silent witnesses: The court system and people who use nonspeech communication. *Talking Politics, 1* (3).

Crossley, R. (1991). Facilitated communication training. *Communicating Together, 9 (2)*, 20–23.

Crossley, R. (1992). Getting the words out: Case studies in facilitated communication training. *Topics in Language Disorders, 12 (4)*, 46.

Crossley, R. (1992). Lending a hand—a personal account of facilitated communication training. *American Journal of Speech-Language Pathology, 1 (3)*, 15.

Crossley, R. (1993). Flying high on paper wings. *Interchange*. April 1993.

Crossley, R., & McDonald, A. (1980). *Annie's coming out.* Melbourne: Penguin.

Crossley, R., & Remington-Gurney, J. (1992). Getting the words out: Facilitated communication training. *Topics in Language Disorders, 12 (4)*, 29.

Donellan, A., Sabin, L., & Majure, L. (1992). Facilitated communication; beyond the quandry to the questions. *Topics in Language Disorders, 12 (4)*, 69.

Eastham, D., (1992). *Silent words: A biography.* Ottawa: Oliver-Pate.

Farkus, Paul, (1992). Thoughts about myself and my autism. *Communicating Together, 10 (4)*, 15.

Haney, C. (1988). Communication device today, competency tomorrow: Are we being realistic in our expectations. *Assistive Device News, 2*, 5–6.

Intellectual Disability Review Panel (IDRP) (1989). *Report to the director general on the reliability and validity of assisted communication.* Office of Intellectual Disability Services, Melbourne.

Johnson, I. (1988, July). When the pen is mightier than the word. *Community Care, 28.*

Johnson, I. (1989). Hellish difficult to live in this world. *Journal of Social Work Practice, Vol. 4, No.1.*

Johnson, I. (1993, January 7). Free speech. *Social Work Today.*

Koppenhofer, J., Gilmer, D., & McElroy, H. (1990). *Facilitated communication: An annotated anthology,* Orono, Center for Community Inclusion.

McNaughton, S., & Lindsay, P. (1992). Facilitated communication: A good way to travel, a runaway train, or both? *Communicating Together, 10 (4)*, 2.

McPhail, P. (1992).Facilitating technology with FC. *Communicating Together, 10 (4)*, 17.

Nolan, C. (1987). *Under the eye of the clock.* London: Weidenfeld and Nicolson.

Pierce, C., & Tweedie, G. (1992). Facilitated communication and preschoolers; Our experience. *Communicating Together, 10 (4)*, 13.

Prior, R, & Cummins, M. (1992). Questions about facilitated communication and autism, *Journal of Autism and Developmental Disorders, 22 (3)*, 331.

Remington-Gurney, J. (1991, Winter). Facilitated communication in mainstream schools. *Australian Communication Quarterly, 6.*

Remington-Gurney, J. (1992). Katie's story. *Communicating Together, 10 (4),* 16.

Schalow, A., & Schalow, A. (1985). The endless search for help. In M. Brady & P. Gunther (Eds.), *Integrating moderately and severely handicapped learners: Strategies that work.* Springfield, IL: Charles C. Thomas.

Swerissen, H., & Newton, J. (1989). *Facilitated augmentative and alternative communication in natural settings by people assessed as having an intellectual disability.* Unpublished paper, La Trobe University, Melbourne.

Szempruch, J., & Jacobson, J., (1993). Evaluating facilitated communications of people with developmental disabilities, *Research in Developmental Disabilities, 14,* 253–264

Woods, E. (1992). "i not handicapped in my brain." *Clinical Management, 12 (3),* 28.

About the Author

Rosemary Crossley has worked with people with severe communication impairments since the early 1970's. In 1977, while working at St. Nicholas Hospital (a state institution for children diagnosed as severely and profoundly retarded) she taught a group of teenagers with cerebral palsy to communicate through spelling using a technique which has since become known as facilitated communication. In 1979 Anne McDonald, her first student, went to the Supreme Court of Victoria to win her freedom from the hospital, and Anne and Rosemary later coauthored a book, *Annie's Coming Out*. The film based on the book was released in the U.S. under the title *Test of Love*.

In 1985 Federal and State governments jointly funded the establishment of DEAL, the first center in Australia devoted solely to the needs of people with severe communication impairments, and Rosemary became its first Director. The Centre employs a multidisciplinary team who provide augmentative communication assessment and training to anyone with a severe expressive communication impairment. Clients include individuals with developmental disabilities such as cerebral palsy and autism, and acquired conditions such as traumatic brain damage, cerebrovascular accidents, and amyotrophic lateral sclerosis.

Rosemary writes and makes conference presentations on aspects of augmentative and facilitated communication. In second semester 1992 she was a visiting scholar at Syracuse University, teaching a course in augmentative communication. She was awarded the Order of Australia in 1986 for services to people with communication impairments.

Index

⊷ ⊷ ⊷ ⊷

148

Index

Low muscle tone (cont'd.)
  definition of, 136
  management of, 58–59
  people with, seating for, 49–50

M
Makaton sign vocabulary, 3, 125
Manual sign, 10–11
McDonald, A., 130
McNaughton, S., 1
Meaning, clarification of, by receiver, 44
Message passing, as method of validation, 97
Missing letters, in words, replacement of, 30
Misunderstandings, 105–110
Monitoring
  of communication, by receiver, 43
  of eye contact, 138
  of output, 138
Multiple choice questions, 30
Multiple choice tests, 76–77
Muscle instability
  radial/ulnar, 23–24, 136–137
Muscle strength, development and maintenance of, 52
Muscle tone
  definition of, 133–134
  high, 20, 136
  low. See Low muscle tone
My Talking Computer, 81–83, 115, 126

N
Neuromotor impairments
  definition of, 133
  terminology, 133–134
Nonspeech communication, 1–3
  definition of, 132
  limitations of, 102–112
  receivers of, guidelines for, 43–46
  versus speech, 86
  successful, requirements for, 28–29
Nonspeech communication strategies, 10–11
  selection of, 11–12
Nonspeech tests, 76–77

O
Oppenheim, Rosalind, 5
Oral responses, tests requiring, 75–76
Outcomes, with facilitated communication training, 129–130
Output, monitoring of, 138
Output processes, 38
Over-interpretation, avoidance of, 138

P
Parsons, C. L., 125
Participation, and muscle strength, 52
Partner influence. See also Receiver
  assessment of, 88–89
Patience, of receiver, 43
Peabody Picture Vocabulary Test, 76–77, 84, 127
Perseveration, 21–22
  definition of, 134, 136
  problems with, and testing, 77
Personal computers, 2
Personnel factors, assessment of, 79
Phonetic spelling, definition of, 132–133
Phonic errors, in word-finding problems, 69
Phrases, common, completion of, 30
Physical performance, 47–56
Pictorial systems, 3
Pointer, versus finger-pointing, 55
Pointing, 17, 47. See also Index finger
  problems with, 53–56
  supports for, 21–22, 60–63
Pointing responses, tests requiring, 76–77
Pointing skills, improvement of, 53–56
Police v. Williams, 96
Poor eye-hand coordination, 19
  definition of, 136
  management of, 54–56, 58
  and testing, 77
Position, and level of independence, 59
Possum scanning typewriter, 2
Postural stability, and seating, 48–51
Posture, 47–56
Posture cushions, 49–50
Pragmatic skills, 14
  acquisition of, 103
Preliminary screening, for validation testing, 95
Preliminary training, for validation testing, 95–96
Print. See Written language
Proprioception, reduced, 25
  definition of, 137
Proximal instability, 24–25
  definition of, 137
Pull back, 138

Q
Question
  multiple choice, 30
  true/false, 30
  yes/no, 30
Question answering, 30
Questioning, informal, assessment of facilitator's skills with, 94